Gifts of Gravity and Light

Gifts of Gravity and Light

A Nature Almanac for the 21st Century

Edited by Anita Roy and Pippa Marland

HODDER

First published in Great Britain in 2021 by Hodder & Stoughton
An Hachette UK company

This paperback edition published in 2022

1

A CIP catalogue record for this title is available from the British Library

Paperback ISBN 9781529363197
eBook ISBN 9781529363173

Typeset in Bembo by Hewer Text UK Ltd, Edinburgh
Printed and bound in Great Britain by Clays Ltd, Elcograf S.p.A.

Hodder & Stoughton policy is to use papers that are natural, renewable
and recyclable products and made from wood grown in sustainable
forests. The logging and manufacturing processes are expected to
conform to the environmental regulations of the country of origin.

Hodder & Stoughton Ltd
Carmelite House
50 Victoria Embankment
London EC4Y 0DZ

www.hodder.co.uk

Contents

Foreword

Bernardine Evaristo

My white mother wanted to raise her mixed-race children in the English countryside, where we could run free. She'd spent some of her childhood in rural Norfolk as an evacuee during the war. Away from the bombing of London, living in a cottage surrounded by fields, it had been idyllic and instilled in her a longing to return. My mother was also realistic, however, and she worried about the racism we'd face if we left the city walls. London it was to be. The suburb of Woolwich, to be precise, in the sixties and seventies. Luckily, there was a common at the end of our road, smaller parks in the area and we had a large and wild garden.

The first time I left London was aged eight on a family holiday to the Devon coast to visit my mother's friend from her college days. My lasting memory of the trip is that her children were horrible to us and called us monkeys. I didn't venture into the English countryside again until I was at college and spent a day on a Yorkshire moor during a field trip. I vividly recall quietly slipping away from the group, climbing to the top of a small mound shrouded in mist and spinning with my arms out while a light splatter of rain fell

vii

on my face. It was an exhilarating, spiritual, private experience as I connected to the countryside for the first time in my life. A few years later, touring with my theatre company, we sometimes lodged in rural areas. When our troupe of black actresses walked into local pubs, they fell silent. We were aliens in their midst and made to feel unwelcome. The message was to go back to where we came from – London.

It is different today, of course; country dwellers are usually more enlightened, and I have learned to be more entitled about claiming ownership of the country of my birth. I haven't encountered any hostility for decades but still, rural England remains under-explored for me, just as I'm sure it is for many people of colour. The generation who settled in Britain after the war did so in the metropolis, where there was more employment. The countryside remained predominantly white.

The nature that inspires me most, the landscapes and seascapes that are flamboyant and panoramic on a grand scale, are to be found abroad. I am more interested in the drama and, I admit, exoticism of the natural world than the minutiae of it. My travels in Africa have taken me to the Sahara, forests, savannahs, islands and lakes. In Brazil I sailed down the Amazon for a week and I love the luxuriantly tropical vegetation of hot countries. Italian and Swiss mountains are favourites, as is the Mediterranean coast. The geysers of Iceland are an unforgettable natural phenomenon, and I once spent ten days dog-sledding on the ice in Greenland (as passenger, not driver, I must add), miles away from any settlements, with only a brilliant blue sky and icebergs on the horizon. It was the most extraordinary experience – no buildings, no plants, no birds, no animals except for the seals, which my hosts hunted for our meals. I felt completely at one with my environment and myself and entered a meditative state. On reflection, travel and nature are intertwined for me. Rejected on home turf at a young, formative age, I turned elsewhere, and found it more exciting.

As a Londoner, I enjoy and need its canals and parks for my cycle rides and walks. I would not be able to breathe if I could not escape man-made constructions. When I do leave the city, when I find myself on the English coast or in woods, walking across fields or climbing hilly paths, I relish it, feel reinvigorated, promise myself to discover more of the nature in my own country. I take the countryside back with me to London and keep it alive inside me for as long as I can. My ideal home would position London at my back door, with a view of mountains and the sea from the front. It's a recurring fantasy.

When I think of nature writing, I have in my head the prevailing image of the great white, privately educated male bestriding the hills and fells of Ye Olde Engla-land. He is considered the authority on the land and indeed for much of history, he owned it, and I think, still does to this day. His property, his domain. Women could become land-owners if single or widowed, but until 1882, the property of any woman who married was automatically transferred to the husband. And while the men in the family were most likely to inherit land, primogeniture meant women usually did not. Only after the 1925 Law of Property Act came into force in 1926 could all women enjoy the same legal rights to own land as men.

It really is time to wrest the writing of nature away from those who have dominated it for so long. Elizabeth-Jane Burnett's nature memoir, *The Grassling* (2019), is one such intervention. Burnett is witness to the countryside from her perspective as a mixed-race woman. She immerses us deeply into the natural world of Devon where she grew up and she stakes her claim to rural England. The book is quite groundbreaking considering that most black British literature has been confined to life inside the conurbation.

Gifts of Gravity and Light also makes an important contribution to the field of nature writing with multiple perspectives and experiences expanding and enriching its possibilities, thereby replenishing the genre. The contributors are predominantly female and drawn from a range of backgrounds. The anthology takes us through the seasons, from spring through to winter, while also taking us around the world: England, Cambodia, India, Zimbabwe, Indonesia, Australia, Belgium, France, Jamaica, Scotland, Wales. We read about the interconnectivity between the natural world and social, cultural, political and personal narratives and history. The essays are far-reaching and raise questions around gender, sexuality and race, alongside ruminations on the earth's origins and migration stories, and issues around biculturalism. I learned something new from each enjoyable essay and by the end realised that nature is integral to how we live on this planet; not a subsidiary to life, but at the heart of it.

The built environment is, of course, essential, but we urgently need to find creative ways for nature to coexist – and indeed flourish – alongside it. The natural world is the life force literally rolling with gravitational force beneath our feet.

Promise

Remember, the time of year
when the future appears
like a blank sheet of paper
a clean calendar, a new chance.
On thick white snow

you vow fresh footprints
then watch them go
with the wind's hearty gust.
Fill your glass. Here's tae us. Promises
made to be broken, made to last.

— Jackie Kay

SPRING

The Wishing Dance

Kaliane Bradley

When I was a child, my parents took me, my sisters and my best friend to a New Year's Eve party held at Walthamstow Town Hall. The town hall is a beautiful, gaunt 1930s building, with an enormous blue fountain in front of it. The year I was there, the weather was so cold that the water had iced over. I'd never seen so much natural ice in one place before, and my friend and I walked along the edge with one foot on the flagstones and the other tottering along the ice. After about a dozen steps, my foot went right through.

When the time came to mark the transition from old year to new, we stood inside the hall and hooted along with all the adults when balloons dropped from the ceiling. In the moment they fell, I forgot all about my uncomfortably cold, wet foot, the tethered sensations of my body. The rain of balloons was the most thrilling thing I'd seen in my life. It was as if the broad nets swathing the ceiling had been holding all the potential of the new year against the stucco; when midnight struck, it rained down on us.

That night impressed on me the importance of marking the time and the turning years. I'd never really understood, before that night, that the new year could promise *freshness*, perhaps because I was so young myself. I saw then, though, that ritual can sometimes be a chance to consciously invite a clear, clean newness in — although at the time, this was thought as, 'Wow! Cool balloons!'

The spark of the ritual dissipates quickly. Every January, I watch the 'Happy New Year!' email openings wither away as workloads frost screens. Towards the end of the month, I'm occasionally hailed with 'Happy Lunar New Year!' which is a nice excuse to talk about my zodiac sign (dragon), but I find that people are simply hoping that emails find me well by the time Valentine's Day comes around.

It is a great deal of fun to horrify my correspondents by opening with 'Happy Cambodian New Year' each April, just when they thought they were safe from seasonal greetings.

Choul Chnam Thmey ('Enter the New Year') is, like many new year festivals that follow the solar cycle, both a harvest festival and a religious one. It falls just before the long rainy season. In Cambodia, it is celebrated over the course of several days, and includes traditional games, foods, songs, dances, and offerings to ancestors and to the Buddha, via his monk intermediaries. In the UK, where the population of the diaspora is approximately 1,000 people, it tends to take place over the course of one afternoon — or at least, it did for my family.

For years, my mother was a president of CASUNIK, the National Lottery-funded society of Cambodians living in the United Kingdom. Every spring, CASUNIK's committee organised a new year's celebration at what was once known as the Vietnamese, Laotian and Cambodian (VLC) Refugee Centre in Haggerston. If you remember the village hall of your childhood – that small stage, those polished floors, the high windows in the plain white walls – then you have an accurate picture of what the VLC Centre's main hall looked like. On the day, there would be prayers from the monks from Amaravati Temple, followed by food offerings and a general buffet; then a show of arts and music; then, in the evening, a raffle and a disco. For as long as my mother was president, and in fact for a few years afterwards, I was part of the show. Every year I would perform a solo version of Robam Chuon Por, the Blessing or Wishing Dance.

Robam Chuon Por is performed at celebrations at which it might be appropriate to lay goodwill upon the audience – it's not exclusively a New Year dance, and I was once or twice called upon to appear at weddings. It is danced in full apsara regalia, into which I had to be sewn an hour before my performance, culminating with Buddhist prayers and the placing of the stacked golden headdress, which resembles the spires of ancient temples. It required weeks of dedicated coaching from my dance teacher, who was herself a former member of Cambodia's Royal Ballet and once performed with the Princess Buppha Devi, the great prima ballerina of the Royal Ballet of Cambodia, whose performances revitalised the form of Cambodian classical dance. (My dance teacher's daughter is the only other person I know who shares my first name, and dance training always meant a chance to hang out with the 'other Kaliane', who

I remember as a tomboyish girl who loved Peter Andre.) And it required flowers.

It is seared into my cerebellum; I cannot hear the opening chords without my muscle memory flickering into life like an old projector. And I cannot see spring blossoms on the trees of London without thinking about the duty to which I was bound, which I abandoned when I was seventeen.

Cambodian classical dance bears a sculptural resemblance to the classical dances of India, but is performed at a much slower, meditative pace. Visually, it is similar to Thai classical dance, although for a long and happy life I advise never saying that to a Thai or Cambodian person. It evokes the carvings of apsara dancers on the walls of Angkor Wat, and, when done well, is an extraordinarily beautiful, lyrical thing.

Robam Chuon Por is about eight minutes long and peaks when the dancer or dancers reach into the golden or silver goblets they carry, fingers pinched like closed lotus flowers, and pluck out blossoms to scatter gracefully at their feet, blessing the audience. (It is not considered elegant to hurl the blossoms overarm to make sure everyone gets blessed.) I always imagined that the sight was very like watching a tree spirit shake her branches and drop her largesse. The blossoms fell like a springtime snow.

For the act to be really beautiful, the blossoms need to be as fresh as possible. This meant that the last thing I would do before taking my place in the tiny wings of the VLC Centre's tiny stage was rush out onto the streets of Haggerston with my mum, my dad and my sisters – tottering a little because of my costume – and grab a couple of fistfuls of blossom off the cherry trees. Poor trees! We'd tumble frantically over the street looking for the fullest and pinkest flowers, selecting two or three from each tree. My dad, almost a foot taller than my mum, was usually able to reach the nicest ones.

The trees were always in bloom because it was always April. They never let me down; they were so constant I never had cause to think about how grateful I should be that they were always able to help me. In recent years, I've watched the street trees outside my bedroom window put out their pinks as early as January, and the full green flush seems to come earlier every spring. I don't know how the trees outside the VLC Centre are faring. Could a dancer still get the blossoms she needed by mid-April, or would she have to resort to the plastic blooms in the buckets at Homebase?

You never realise what lifelong habits are crystallising inside you while they are forming, but once they're embedded, they build bones in the soul of you. I wasn't so aware of the potency of the ritual when I was training to dance and plundering trees, experiencing it only as a task to complete, but of course it plaited itself into my body. Now, the ritual is sunk into me, triggered every spring when the trees bloom. Every time I see the pink lacework on trees, I am reminded of my duty to the season. When the blossoms are unseasonable, it engenders a feeling of dread in me similar to sensing the first hot and morbid congestion of a nosebleed. As I write this, in the second national lockdown of 2020, my mother has texted me a picture of the tree at the end of my parents' road in South Woodford. 'This tree must be very confused!! because it blossoms now!!!' It is four months early, and is yet to endure the January frosts. I hate living through unprecedented times, with all the rituals that hold us coming unstuck.

Spring rituals are my favourites because the cold is my enemy and the darkness makes a clown of me; in this I am separated from the seasons of Cambodia (hot-wet, hot-dry) and the Buddhist festivals of Vesak, in April, and Kathina, in October, which follow the rains. My body grew up in a European temperate climate and so, like a plant, I bend to the environment around me. I engage with British seasons in primary colours, like a small child. I love big phallic maypoles and their split skirts of ribbons. I love the flowered headdresses that transform every woman into a sacrificial maiden. I especially love to remind the people around me that spring rituals were held with a kind of bacchanal desperation. O Green Man! O Demeter! O Piper at the Gates of the Seasons! We thank you for this gift of flowers, we thank you for the warming days, the golden light! Please, please, give us at least another six months before you take it all away again! The ritual that I love most of all the spring rituals is rarely observed on village greens – the driving of livestock and young men through bonfires for the Gaelic festival of Beltane. It marks the beginning of the summer, and places great faith in the purifying, holy nature of fire. It is only appropriate to be so abject before the elemental violence of the changing seasons that you turn to the flames to face it. This is how I think nature should be spoken to. When nature is the cuddly bunny and the friendly old hill, it becomes too easy to dismiss it as a faithful retainer who will never retire. But nature is the panic at the end of a talon, and it's the tree with a heart of fire where lightning has struck. It is not our friend, and we do not want to make it our enemy.

Without memory of this awe, a fragment of which can be found in the petal of any flower crown, the crudest of paintings on a hen's blown egg, we are unglued from time and space. We do not remember our debts to the world around us, and we use it like a napkin. I have lived all of my life in cities, and am reliant on the structure of ritual to keep my body in sync with the seasons. I work at a computer and I live in a country where I can buy strawberries in November. Without ritual, I go through time encased in artificial lukewarm plastic. I might as well be buried. A friend of mine told me that he'd started writing a difficult chapter of his thesis just as the summer was ending and the university term was starting. By the time he'd worked his way through the problems and typed the data set, the trees were bare and the sky was iron every morning. 'And just like that, I realised I'd missed autumn,' he said.

I'm very worried that one day, I'll look out of the window and realise I've missed the spring. That I'll have travelled so far from the living world around me, so deep into a screen, I'll have forgotten to honour it. That I'll have forgotten to honour it, and so be rid of the ghostly tug of guilt I feel every year when I see spring blossoms and remember I stopped dancing. That I'll have shrugged off the guilt, and with it, shrugged off an integral part of me that is Cambodian.

An important thing to consider about rituals is who they are for, viz., it was certainly not for the tree that I was pulling out blossoms, but for the people in the VLC Centre and especially for my mother. A tree couldn't care less what humans are writing about it in their poetry and their songs. Probably trees have their own songs.

It's easy for trees to appear rapturously sacred. Some of them have been around for so long that they've witnessed the work of generations fall and rebuild around them. Every year, as I came bursting out of the VLC Centre, I thought they looked like sentinels of the season, standing on the street. I've conscripted them into my army of images. In writing this essay, I am crudely hanging my thoughts and feelings about all sorts of themes – climate catastrophe, identity and its crises, and, in a few paragraphs, inevitably, the genocide – over their branches like so much tossed toilet roll. Their presence, I argue, brings me closer to nature, but what if it's putting another barrier in the way? Poetry about daffodils on a hill is all very well but it has nothing on the miracle of photosynthesis.

Put it this way: one summer evening, I was discussing nature writing, in the context of reincarnation, with my friend Anna, who is herself a talented writer whose thoughts about memory and ritual have often informed my own. I believe in reincarnation, because I was brought up a Buddhist and it seems as good an answer as any for what happens to the soul once the body lets it go. I have never been able to disabuse myself of the notion of a soul; please don't try, I had a very sad and stressful time trying to do it to myself when Richard Dawkins was popular in the early noughties and religious people were considered, broadly speaking, fucking idiots.

I was explaining to Anna that I think I'm on my first incarnation as a human, and this would explain why I have so much trouble tackling the normal human range of emotions. It feels as if there's too much happening simultaneously. I am probably used to being a sea cucumber or something.

Anna is a supportive friend and exists in the world in an exceptionally empathetic way; whatever her personal beliefs, she believes I believe in mine. She said that she found herself disengaged when nature writing focused on (e.g.) a bird in the garden, alighting in a bush and singing its marvellous, bittersweet song before flying off, making the writer think (e.g.) about the sumptuous and generous beauty of the natural world. 'But that bird is an individual,' she said. 'It's not a symbol, it's a bird among birds. To other birds, it's a particular bird. It's not a vehicle for our feelings about it.' I agreed enthusiastically – I'd drunk the larger share of our bottle of wine — and said that the bird might one day be your niece, your lover, your horrible boss.

It seems foolish to observe it, but if I don't, I forget it: our rituals around the seasons — the harvest, the rains, the lengthening dark — do not so much commune with nature as commune with one another. We don't celebrate the arrival of spring in order to welcome spring through the door, pouring fresh sunlight into the cobwebby corners, though it can be pleasurable to imagine this. Spring will come whether we call it or not. But we can fall into step with the spring, making our own motions that mirror the deep magic of putting out flowers. After all, it's us and our trees, mushrooms, bugs and animals against the big dead maw of the universe outside. This is also why, every year, when the high saturation images of blossoms against sugary blue skies arrive in their dozens on Instagram, I slam that heart on every single one.

It is often remarked that travel writing is always, ulti-mately, about the writer's home, and all forms of travel are a method of homecoming and home recollection. I think the same is true of nature writing. Each time I've tried to access the sorcery and strangeness of spring blossoms, their simultaneous existence as arboreal phenomena and photo opportunity, I find myself trying to explain Cambodia, or trying to explain the Wishing Dance. As I'm doing right now, against my best intentions, I always find myself trying to explain *me*.

It's true, too, that whenever I think about the rituals of spring, celebrating the stirring of new life, it's because I'm thinking about the death that sits flush against it, flank to flank. The shimmering cycle of living and departing feels coherent and honourable when I think about it as 'nature'; it takes the fear out of thinking about death; I go to the fragments of the natural world with which I'm familiar when I'm trying to keep myself from getting the vertigo I experience when I think about what dying is like, is going to be like. Consider the bird on your bird feeder. Consider the sparrow. This individual sparrow is one of 10 million in the UK, which sounds like a lot, but it is 20 million fewer than we had in 1966; 20 million little hearts that never started beating! What an essay I could start with a line like that!

It's an unfathomable number, but it's a good place to begin, before I start building up to bigger bodies. An estimated 1.5 to 2 million people died during Pol Pot's Khmer Rouge regime, about a quarter of Cambodia's population at the time. Among them were my grandparents, several of my uncles and aunts, and my cousins. One of my uncles lost his first wife and all of his children but one, sparrow by sparrow, and had to keep on living afterwards. My mother has regretted throwing away her father's letters for decades – she thought she was going to see him again in a few years, couldn't have imagined how long 'never again' would be. They were all individuals among individuals. I struggle to fathom; I stare at the bird feeder; I think, as a greyish sadness rises, as hard as I can about the blossoms of the trees, which come back every year, trees hinting in cryptic clues at the deathless cycle of nature, seeming to promise that the souls of the unjustly murdered found new homes in next lives.

London is one of the leafiest cities in the world. There are almost as many trees as there are Londoners. As a teenager, growing up in South Woodford – very far north – I lived on the tamer edges of Epping Forest. The trees had been there quite a lot longer than I had, and I hope they will be there quite a lot longer after I'm gone, though they are sectioned by motorways, cul-de-sacs and the inevitable bloody golf courses.

Hackney and Haggerston have an incredibly diverse range of trees, planted deliberately by the council. I can just about recognise pear and cherry blossoms, but there are plum, pear, olive and almond trees out there too. The trees closest to the VLC Centre were cherry trees. Like most cherry trees in cities, they have been chosen for their flowers rather than their fruit, which only the birds are likely to enjoy.

My concept of 'nature' and the 'natural world' has mostly been curated for me by urban human experience. Trees push the prices of houses up on streets where they grow (something which, if I think about it for too long, makes me dissociate – the trees never asked to be implicated in our unhinged property market). We are advised to go out into 'nature' and be contiguous with it for the good of our mental health. We are soothed by the eternal silent sagacity

of the trees even as we might stress out 'nature' around us
– I think gloomily of stories of Epping Forest being over-
foraged; of the great green deserts created for golf; of the
day ramblers who, in the absence of bins, drop their plastic,
leave banana skins to rot against walls; of sheep chewing
through the hills and growing Christmas jumpers on their
backs. It's difficult to shake the feeling that my relationship
with the natural world is that of a coloniser. It makes it
harder to interrogate my relationship with the land, which
in turn complicates my relationship with the concept of
country.

When you lose a land – as I have, I suppose, lost one,
without ever having known it – it becomes a mystical,
antediluvian place, sustained by legend, by story, and every
flower in it glows with magical intent. My mum has a lot
of good stories about what life was like in pre-Khmer
Rouge Cambodia. There are some that make the rounds
every other time we have a glass of wine together. One of
my favourites is the story of the boat buffet.

When my mum talks to me about the family I never
knew, she uses the term 'grandfather' interchangeably, to
mean the man who adopted her or the man to whom she
was born. The two men had married sisters and were both
important figures in Cambodian politics, so they were
family, and their social and professional lives overlapped in
a Venn diagram that was an almost perfect circle. This has,
in the past, been confusing, because it means I have heard
stories about my 'grandfather' in which he appears to
undergo a personality transplant: my grandfather, the

austere colonel, a devout Buddhist brought up by monks, who could make grown men vibrate with terror in his presence; my grandfather, the extravagant eccentric, who threw some of Phnom Penh's wildest parties and was briefly imprisoned for using public money to build a bridge that finished halfway across a river.

The boat buffet story is one from the eccentric grandfather repertoire.

My grandfather owned some land outside Phnom Penh, in a village called Kdei Takoy, along the banks of the River Mekong. The earth there was wet and heavy, frequently flooding in the rainy season. The local people lived in stilted houses. (My mum describes them as 'the people who looked after the land' – were they employed by my grandfather to take care of the land, or was he their landlord? She cannot say for sure.) Phka snao (*Sesbania bispinosa*) flourished in green, prickling clumps, dense as a forest. When the land flooded, they appeared to grow directly out of the water, their complex little yellow flowers hanging like bells.

These flowers are edible. Like courgette flowers, they can be fried in a batter. My grandfather came up with a brilliant idea: they would take boats out into the flooded land, with portable cooking equipment, and fry the flowers on the bow. Phka snao has twiny stems, easily bent under pressure. It would be plain sailing.

There were three boats – long, flat-bottomed traditional boats equipped with puttering motors and an oar for emergencies. They bobbed along in a row. In the first boat were a couple of servants, whose job was to grab the flowers and dunk them in the batter before releasing them. In the second were my grandfathers, my great-uncle and their wives, reaching out to pluck the pkha snao; they ate them with dipping sauce and fresh vegetables. My mum and her siblings were in the third (children's) boat, picking up the tail of the feast.

'It was wonderful,' my mum says to me. 'But your grandfather was like that. He enjoyed to have a good time.'

I love this story for numerous reasons. I love it because it's a happy, idyllic story, and I like to think that at least part of my mum's youth was happy and idyllic, before Lon Nol, before Pol Pot. I love it because it's a story about food, and I like thinking about food. But I also love it because it's a story about the land itself.

It's a nostalgic story about a land that my mother lost, which, even in present day Cambodia, cannot ever be returned to her; the boats through the phka snao are a sign that she once belonged to and was sustained by that land. But it's a story filled with unattested narrative too. Who were the people who lived there all year round? And the servants? Were the flowers theirs, too? In a way, it's a story about my grandfather asserting the luxury of ownership. *This is my land. I offer its jewels to you, as is my right.*

In 1860, the French explorer Henri Mouhout was introduced to the overgrown ruins of Angkor Wat in what is persistently, bafflingly referred to as a discovery – though Mouhout himself was baffled by the thought that the barbaric Khmers could have built such a magnificent structure. Cambodia was made a protectorate of the French empire in 1863, and the stripping of Angkor Wat's forest cloak began in earnest at the end of the nineteenth century. Of the entire Angkor Archaeological Park, which includes Angkor Wat, Angkor Thom, and the spun sugar stones of Banteay Kdei, only the ruins of Ta Prohm still wear their trees. They curl up through the roofs and drape their roots like languid elder gods, frozen in the middle of an ancient parliament. They have no opinion on the felling of their brothers.

It would have been a crime, a sort of cultural devastation by omission, not to uncover the ruin of Angkor – to drag the forest off it – once the Europeans had been so kind as to discover it for the Khmer people. But the trees of Ta Prohm are melancholy things. They are like the honoured artists of a dying form. I am irresistibly drawn towards comparing them to the second-generation members of the diaspora who are still learning the classical forms of dance, which the Khmer Rouge regime tried to wipe out, but I'll resist it today. Cambodia's primary rainforest cover has dropped from 70 per cent to 3 per cent in fifty years, and the logging trade is corrupt and barely regulated. Every other tree in the country is a commodity. The land has a price. Even when we say we want to preserve nature, we're naming a price.

A personal quirk about my belief in reincarnation is that, if it does exist, I can't imagine it follows linear, chronological time. After all, time is just another dimension, a fluke of the latticework in this universe, and even within this universe the existence of black holes has demonstrated how functionally fragile time is. By contrast, the soul, if it does exist, is eternal, innate, outside of the daub and wattle of the universe's rules. So it should be possible for me to be born before myself. It should be possible, technically, for me to be reborn as a young tree, on a street or in an ancient forest. It is possible for the tree that offered me flowers on the street outside the VLC Centre to have been me, and that I am nature and I am in nature and I observe nature and am observed in nature. It is possible for nature writing to be autobiography. But it's also just as true, and honourable, that the tree is just a tree.

I push myself to remember this every time I read a news headline about unprecedented wildfires, or the pollution of a natural water source for the sake of a pipeline. These acts of seeming deformity are enclosed by the system we have created and operate, believing ourselves to be outside of nature, answerable only to the concepts of 'profit' and 'progress'. I have to remember that poverty and privation are real and appalling, but that the world has enough space for all of us, because we are the world and we have always belonged here.

When I eventually leave this body, I will finally be free, for however long it takes before the next rebirth, of my anthropocentric point of view. What were previously distinct species and experiences will prove to be, as the Buddha tells us, so much sea foam. A tree and I will be the same and we will be neither tree nor woman. We will dance the same dance, simultaneously, along the paths of light and matter that make up reality.

Equinox: I Put this Moment

Pippa Marland

'I put this moment . . . here'
– Kate Bush, 'Jig of Life'

Living in a city, it can be hard to track the turning of the year.
Time passes and my dream of a rustic smallholding with
beehives, a vegetable plot, and a cast of wild, nonhuman
characters still burns brightly in my imagination but recedes
ever further from my grasp, so I attach myself instead to the
places within reach. It's useful for the city dweller to develop
an affection for modest landscapes, for corners that even the
most voracious developer has had to leave be. Sometimes it's
because they mask a disused landfill site so unregulated in its
time that it can never be dug up for fear of what monsters of
toxicity it might unleash, or because their slopes drop so
sharply down the hillside only feral goats can set up home
there. Sometimes they're simply in between uses – their
green resurgence a temporary stay of execution – or, if they're
lucky, they've come under the protection of a local conser-
vation group. They're the places, more than the grander city
parks that have so often been manicured and tamed, where
you can find a little piece of wildness.

The area I visit most often to mark the changing seasons is Bishop's Knoll, a stretch of woodland on the side of the Avon Gorge in Bristol, and below it the meadowlands of Bennett's Patch and White's Paddock. To me, it's a calming place in which the pressures of daily life can be punctuated and paused, though at first sight it might seem a strange choice for someone trying to step outside the headlong rush of time. On its southwest side is the busy Portway, which carries a constant two-way flow of traffic between the city centre and the M5 motorway so that, even in the heart of the woods, you hear the noise of engines. The woodland and the meadow are separated by the Severn Beach railway line, and from the lower ground you can look up and wave at the sparsely occupied, three-carriage trains as they go down towards Temple Meads or out to the coast.

It's not just these markers of our own time that make their presence felt. Bishop's Knoll is thick with history. A deer park in the Middle Ages, the land was given by Henry VIII to his loyal supporter Sir Ralph Sadler after the disso-lution of the monasteries. A grand house called The Knoll was built here in the late nineteenth century, and during the First World War it was converted by its then owner, Robert Bush, a Bristolian who had spent many years as a sheep farmer in Australia, into a hospital for Australian soldiers. His daughter remembered how he would go to the station to meet the trains carrying the wounded from the Front, and search the lines of stretchers for Australians to take back to The Knoll. The house was demolished in

1973, but the gardens, falling steeply down to the meadow-land, remain. The trees bear witness to the landscape's former glory; alongside the path above the railway stand a Monterey cypress, an Oriental spruce, a Corsican pine, a western red cedar, and a coast redwood, their vast trunks soaring into the sky.

Stepping into the woods can be disorienting: suddenly it's hard to tell not just where, but *when* you are. The frame of an old glasshouse pokes brokenly through the brambles, rusted fencing lies here and there in the undergrowth, and the winding paths are thronged with laurel, ivy and bamboo. In parts of the grounds you could believe that no one had set foot there for half a century. But there are signs of recent activity too: new steps cut into the slopes; an orchard cleared and replanted; a children's den among the bushes; a stone wall beautifully repaired. The site is gradually being restored by the Woodland Trust and its volunteers, and the meadows below, previously a neglected sports ground, are in the hands of the Avon Wildlife Trust. Each spring and summer there are more wildflowers, more butterflies. Little by little, I am getting to know the place. There's the nuthatch tree – you hear their strident *bee-bee-bee-bee-bee-bee-beep* before you see them going up and down the trunk – and the branch where the song thrush likes to sing as the light fades. Once, on the upper path, I found the tiny body of a blue tit; I picked it up and gently turned it over, recoiling at the sight of a large tick attached to its head. Another kind of wildness. And down by the railway bridge, close to where I saw the fledgling wrens last year, adult birds are nesting again. Familiarity breeds a complicated, slow-burning sort of love.

Coming here to note the seasonal round, I've been thinking about how the different strands of time – human and nonhuman, linear and cyclical – meet in this deep, rich place. Hidden away in the higher reaches of the wood there's a seven-hundred-year-old sessile oak that was already well grown when Henry VIII's men were tearing down the abbeys, already growing old when wounded Australian soldiers were convalescing under its boughs, and still it endures today. Its slow patience contrasts with the rush of human time registered here – the trains rattling along according to the timetables of the Great Western Railway, the cars and lorries on the Portway with their own deadlines for departure and arrival. And just beyond the road runs the River Avon, rising and falling with the tides as it flows towards Avonmouth, where its waters are caught up in one of the largest tidal variations in the world – second only to the Bay of Fundy in Canada. Here, at the side of the meadows, the tides are marked by water brimming at the river's banks twice a day, reduced to slick patterned mud and a thin brown channel in the hours between.

A walker new to the area might startle as they cross the railway bridge and turn down onto the lower ground. Beside the fence that divides the nature reserve from the

Portway are two huge creatures. Come closer. A humpback whale is breaching the surface, its head rising above the grass, while only the tail and flukes of a blue whale are visible as it dives below. If you were far out at sea, gazing from the deck of a boat, seeing either one of these would be an 'oh' moment of heart-thudding wonder. Here, that sense of enchantment is tempered by the uncanny awareness that the whales are breaching not ocean, but earth. Come closer still. The whales are made of willow on a metal frame. They were created in 2015 to celebrate Bristol's year as the European Green Capital, and displayed in Millennium Square, surrounded by a sea of plastic designed to draw attention to oceanic pollution.

The whales resurfaced at Bennett's Patch a year later, not far from the river that once brought tall ships into the heart of the city. It's not just the strangely exotic trees in the wood that speak of distant countries, of colonialism and empire. Bristol's maritime involvement in trades that still tarnish its name – the wealth it gained from slavery and tobacco – includes a half-century-long excursion into whaling. Just down the Avon from the willow whales, at Sea Mills, their flesh and blood counterparts were unloaded from the whaling ships and their blubber rendered into oil. It can be hard in the city centre to feel the pull of the tides. In the early nineteenth century a dam was built to create the Floating Harbour and the tidal river was diverted along the New Cut to the south. But here on the edge, things feel a little more raw and open. Perhaps it's partly this that draws me to Bishop's Knoll. It's somewhere to stop and rest, but never to escape entirely from a sense of the entanglements of human and natural history.

When we think of 'Time' it sounds monolithic, uniform, the thing that takes us inexorably from the cradle to the grave in an unbroken line, straight as a Roman Road. It stretches unimaginably far behind and ahead of us, framing our brief appearance. But when you look more closely, you see how complex it is – how its many strands weave together and sometimes fray apart. The linear and the cyclical are always moving through and across each other. Take the spring, for example; it returns each year but each time slightly differently. The exact time of the vernal equinox occurs later with each common year and earlier in each leap year, keeping the date on which the northern hemisphere celebrates the start of spring shifting between the 20th and 21st of March. The equinox changes too in relation to the orientation of the earth's axis as it turns through its twenty-six-thousand-year rotation, precessing slowly westwards along the equator across that span of time.

Even when it comes to measuring time, there are variations, different effects that circle round each other. Astronomers have two clocks for earthly days, solar and sidereal, the latter measuring the revolutions of the planet against the fixed stars not the sun. They run at different speeds, in a drifting relation, sometimes coinciding, sometimes not. The fixed stars themselves aren't really fixed, but moving with their galaxies. Time, it seems, is relative throughout the universe. So, a day on Venus – the time the planet takes to turn once on its axis – takes two hundred and forty-three of ours, but a Venusian year is completed in less than two of its own days. Puzzling through this makes my head hurt, but equally it frees me from the feeling that time is bearing down on me, that beyond my own sense of the temporal is a rigid framework boxing me in. There's evidence of such complexity closer to home, though it's so fractional that it passes us by unobserved. Down on Bennett's Patch, because of the effects of local gravity, time is moving more slowly than up in the canopy of the woods. But there's also the kind of variation that I can see, laid out before my eyes. The tides of the Avon are altering visibly, every ebb and flow a little different as they move with the gravitational pull and orbital variations of the moon and sun, with barometric pressure, and with the changing bathymetry of the Bristol Channel. On a graph, the patterns of the river's rise and fall look like the open mouth of a white shark, bristling with jagged points and deep, uneven troughs.

We humans have our own cyclical renewals, physically and emotionally, never twice the same as we move through the days, weeks, months and seasons of each succeeding year. Our cells replace themselves; we find ourselves in the light again after long spiritual darkness. Like elderberry wine that starts re-fermenting at the time of year the berries first ripened and were picked, our bodies remember the seasons and dance to their rhythms in ways we can

sometimes articulate, but more often cannot. We're complicated — temporally and materially chimeric creatures that
carry, in the very matter that makes up our bodies, both
recent and deep time, intimate cellular connections and
cosmic atomic entanglements. It's become almost a cliché
to acknowledge the micro-organisms that make us all
inherently plural; they live on and inside us, festooning our
eyelashes, nestling into the crooks of our elbows, and clus-
tering together in our stomachs. But there are other, more
extraordinary inhabitations. When I was pregnant with my
two daughters, the chances are that I experienced microchimerism — cells from the babies I was carrying would
likely have crossed the placenta and spread through my
body. Their cells would have travelled to different organs,
and any that went into my heart, for example, would have
developed into cardiac tissue and become a part of my own
beating heart. The word chimera comes from Greek
mythology, from the monstrous dragon/goat/lion hybrid,
and I can see how that would fit here: researchers believe
that the foetal cells might influence the mother's own biology, sometimes to their own advantage and, possibly, the
detriment of the mother. It's wildly strange to think of it
— part terrifying *Alien* territory, part utter, overwhelming
beauty.

At the other end of the scale from this most intimate of
hybridities is the idea that we each carry the matter of the
stars within us. From the Renaissance onwards, astronomers began to understand the material nature of celestial
bodies, including the realisation that stars were 'things' that

could die, sometimes spectacularly. With that knowledge came the apprehension that, as the astrophysicist Michel Cassé writes, 'we ourselves are but the dust and ashes of stars'. Human bones contain heavy elements from stars that died billions of years ago; our atoms house the history of the universe. One of the great challenges of our time is to think in thousands and millions of years, an intellectual feat necessary to comprehend the implications of the Anthropocene, both in terms of the vast time spans involved in the making of geological epochs and the horrifying speed, relatively speaking, with which human impacts are beginning to define the new era. Knowing ourselves to be plural material things that have somehow coalesced into the beings we each call 'me', populated by strange tiny animals, by each other, and by the ancient matter of the stars helps us, I think, to understand our complete involvement in the planet, helps us to know more fully what traditional wisdom has long told us: that what we do to the earth, we do to ourselves.

But of course, we are ageing too. Even as the linear and the cyclical are playing themselves out in us in a delicate, complex dance, the linear is starting to lead. As we grow older the internal balance of dark and light is altered, and our innate springtime exuberance becomes a little muted. If my cells entered my mother's body when she was carrying me, they are gone now, dispersed into the earth. I wonder about how the nonhuman world experiences its own entropy. Does the sessile oak at Bishop's Knoll feel its senescence and know its growth rings to be finite? Does it sense the slow thinning of its canopy of leaves, the lesser bounty of its acorns? I once held a blue tit that had been caught, not for the first time, in a ringer's net. The bird hadn't travelled far from the place he had been ringed nine and a half years earlier, making him only two months short of the oldest recorded blue tit in the country. My daughter, standing at my side, said she had never seen a bird that looked so old; he seemed as if he seen things, lived a whole lot of life, and his feathers were a little . . . raddled. I released him in the way I had been instructed, holding him on his back in the palm of my hand with his feet crossed, and then up-cupping him into the air. Did he know that his cyclical round was coming closer to its end? In Bennett's Patch the willow whales – mid-breach, mid-plunge – are ageing too. The willow is rotting and breaking away, to reveal the rusting mesh and poles that make the frames. Wild clematis is weaving through the gaps, and nettles are standing guard within and without the metal skeletons.

So what do we do with this sure sense of our demise? Just sometimes you might stand stock still and something shifts in your spirit and you feel thankful to have made it through. For me, as for others I'm sure, this mostly happens in spring: the sense of a new brightness in the air, the almost-forgotten feeling of the sun's warmth on the body, the slowly creeping green surge through the hedges. The vernal equinox – the day on which the earth's hemispheres are equally illuminated by the sun – is the beginning of my year. The nature writer Tim Dee explains in *Greenery* that the spring travels up from the equator at roughly human walking pace. I imagine it making its UK landfall at Cape Cornwall and stepping over the prone rocks of the Brisons – Charles de Gaulle in profile, lying in the Celtic sea – then heading slowly north. It's not too far up from the Cornish coast to Bishop's Knoll. As the calendar reaches late March you can feel confident in the progress of that greening, and enjoy the excitement of counting the first, the first, the first, the first: chiffchaff; celandine; wood anemone; blue- bell. The deeper winter greens of ivy, laurel, holly and last year's brackish bramble growth are giving way to the lighter shades of hawthorn, hedge parsley and goosegrass.

When I was a child I loved the book *The Secret Garden* by Frances Hodgson Burnett. Inspired by the dawn and the stars and woodland sunsets the narrator says, 'One of the strange things about living in the world is that it is only now and then one is quite sure one is going to live forever and ever and ever.' When I was younger I almost believed it, literally, religiously, and then later I didn't agree with it at all, disliking the – to me – false sentiment. But now, again, I think I know what she means. Or at least, how I might accept and celebrate the idea of it. It's in those extraordi- nary moments that come rarely in a lifetime, when the linear and the cyclical and all that is you fall into balance – a little stasis that opens out into the world and travels effort- lessly across your life in time and space. These moments hold all our years within them, so that I, who am always looking to the lost past or to the future that never arrives, always waiting to become the thing I am, can seize a 'now' out of the headlong flight. Here is my father teaching me to tread so lightly in the woods that we surprise a deer; there is my mother brandishing a trowel and heading for the flower bed. It's cold for March; she's wearing an old green coat and her hair is blowing across her face.

And in this moment I want them to be really here, not in the earth, and me not this middle-aged woman who will cry at emotion whether it's happy or sad, because it's too much anyway, because it breaks through that well-worn 'I'm doing OK' façade, which is actually true but also not true. I guess it's the same for everyone, this ripening into age which is both a hardening and a softening. The days go by, and the years go by, and it doesn't matter so much about anything, in a good way, but also sometimes not; sometimes it's a restriction, an entropy of the self before its time, a disengagement from it all. It takes an effort to be still, to let this moment be what it wants to be. There she is in weak spring sunlight, standing in the garden of a 1930s semi and holding a rabbit close to her chest. She's not sure about rabbits, or pets at all, but the rabbit is snuggling in and they look all right. And there he is another year – he's made a seed drill, there's a robin perched on the spade handle, and he's showing me how to space the spinach seeds and drop them one by one.

What it comes down to is this – this late March morning. I'm on the rough track down the side of Bishop's Knoll where unofficial winter streams have grooved the mud between the stones, through the woods and onto Bennett's Patch and White's Paddock. I sit down on the grass in the meadow and then lie back. There's a damp chill coming up from the ground, but the sun is warm on my face. I'm taking stock, while the year is poised between the linear and the cyclical, hinged between the dark and light. We can't know the equinoxes of our own lives but somehow, in this suspension, all the strands of time braid into one, and we are rooted to the earth and sky. When I step out again, I carry all that I have been and all that I might be, finding new strength among the shoots and whorls of new growth. Here it is: the sessile oak; the nuthatches; the whales; the railway and the busy road; the human and nonhuman histories infiltrating and orbiting around each other; the river brimming and dwindling over and over; and all this time and matter intertwined. Breathe in. Walk on, in renewed commitment to this complicated world.

I put this moment . . . here.

Hoarfrost Butterfly

Testament

Home. 2020. Now.

Scrolling
Quickly
Through the gallery
On an iPhone.

Front room
Feet up
Cheap coffee table.

Moments
Captured in my palm
Too many
Suspended
Out of focus

We don't have to wait
For the perfect
Shot
Frame
Or exposure

There is no cost
To deleting
The digital

No trips to
Boots or the photo shop
Or wherever.

So my phone has thousands
And I rarely sit down
To sift

Day
Month
Year
On screen

The seasons
In thumb-induced flux
A flick-book animation
Of my life.
Time-hopping.

Here everything
Is preserved
Seasons remain
Exactly as first envisioned

Each image
Reappears
Telling us
This
Fragile life
Will stay new
And vivid
And alive

In the flurry
Of smudged faces
Bodies in motion
Forgotten sights
It settles on

My blurred boy
In this very room
Last
Spring.

Calderdale. 2020. April.

The first lockdown is in effect. It's only spring and the year
is already held back. Stuck in the mire of too many events.
All my kids are off school; so I'm trying to work, write, and
take part in perpetual Zoom sessions and attempt parent-
hood at the same time. So the boy is in front of the box. I
think he looks . . .

I smile, lift my phone and press the camera icon.

He is three years old. Wearing the red-and-white-striped hoodie that he will soon grow out of. He is lying across the seat of a chair on his belly ogling the children's TV. I tap on the image and the picture captures him in the soft light that comes through the tall bay window behind him.

I don't notice the trees outside. We've got an evergreen out front. I don't notice the effect the little wayfaring tree is having on my son. It is in flower.

Somewhere between the camera lens and the window's reflection, the plumes of white petals create a ghostly aura of innocence in the scene hanging behind the hooded little boy watching the TV.

It suits him.

Home. 2020. Now.

Freed from the present
Cushioned by so many pictures

Still on the sofa
We only paid off last week.

The boy is now at school.
And our wayfarer outside
Has few green leaves
And looks a little naked.
A different season.
But still
In a small town

In Calderdale.
Funny
I'd always thought
I'd live
In cities.

Decades on from youth
Making a life somewhere
That feels to me
Parochial (though it isn't)

Things bleeding from one time
Into another.
Memory is like that.

Trying to recall
A moment of transition.
When you yourself
Are in transition.

These photos are reminders
To peel back the wallpaper
We get used to.
To see beneath
The imagined.

To me
A season was never finite
Not always annual.

A season of life
Not just
Simply a string of sunny days
Or four quadrants
Or an artist's 'blue period'
Or a playwright's 'seven ages'
But the feeling
Of a phase
Bringing us closer
Or
Pushing farther away.
The objects that centre
Our lives
Warm and cold.
Often full of discomfort
Spring becomes the turning
Of a door on its hinge.

Terraced house, Harehills, Leeds. 2002. April.

I was listening to a laid-back jazz guitar lick in a basement in Harehills. Cousin J's house. Lyric writing. The words would be released on vinyl two springs later. I don't think it was the shadowed, damp surroundings that gave rise to the theme and imagery. The whole network of streets was framed with stoic red-brick terraces, wrought-iron grilles over front doors where the only bits of nature were the hedges that clambered over the short stubby walls separating the front yard from the litter on the pavement. But the air is different, and the sunlight hangs on the doorsteps a little longer.

I eye my biro and rap book, lean over a makeshift desk of breeze blocks, two Yamaha speakers screwed into the beams above us. 'Butterfly'. A stream of consciousness turns into a verse:

Inspiration. I write phrases on the page and
Butterflies flutter by to show there's no danger
I draw close to nature like David Attenborough learning
   animal behaviour
The creator's imprint written in like fate, but
Transform
Lifeform
Forms of life reborn
Cross like the fader
Senses crystallise in chrysalis for respite
Hidden for a season my reason's to grow wise
As I rise in the day taking hold of the twilight
In this urban countryside, love put it right
Like a butterfly

Home. 2020. Now.

It suits him.

But his shifting weight in the chair
Tells me we should get some fresh air.
'A family walk?' We should go for a walk, baby.

Outside a fine day is dimmed. The windowpanes are lazy.
Let's go for another walk. My elbow is tugged.
I'll take the phone with me. 'Cup of tea first, love?'

Pinner, London. 1982. March?

My first recollection of really noticing spring was walking
to school (or was it nursery?) in north London. Over the
cracked asphalt and under cherry blossom trees that burst
into a welcome, promising me that things were going to be
sunnier now. It was the eighties. Only a few blurry photos
with rounded-off edges of the house in Pinner. Dad's hand-
writing on the back tells me that it's 1982. But there's no
month. I'd have been about four or five. We had a few
bushes and a small tree in the front garden. My nostalgia
tells me it always seemed bright and full of flowers. Other
than that I can't remember much about that house. But the
first buds of flower out front remain sweet-smelling residue
in my mind. The secret smile of spring.

It would only be a few years later when my parents saw
an ad in a paper looking for teachers in Zimbabwe: a three-
year contract at Harare High School. Known at that time as
'the breadbasket' of Africa, Zimbabwe was a postcolonial
power coming into its own.

We waved goodbye to the cherry blossom in the front
garden.

Home. 2020. Now.

A thumb
Half a hand
Five out of focus
My three-year-old's chin
You leave them alone for two minutes

Now there's talk
Slight nudges
In temperature
Can change a lot.

A back-and-forth
These islands
Caught between African winds
And the Artic breeze

I hear of a vineyard near me
The Pinot noir grape can now flourish
In England.
Even up here in West Yorkshire

Now there's talk
The great British staple
Tea
Grown on this
Green and pleasant

The great British staple
Small talk about the weather

And the seasons are in conversation
With each other
Trying to work out
What on Earth is going on.

Dewsbury. 1998.

Yorkshire. My DJ friend dubs it 'Tokyorkshire'. The DJ is a Harehills native who now lives in Berlin, but has had a love affair with Japan as long as I've known him. His sound fuses Japanese melodies with the thump of Leeds carnival and the grit of UK hip hop. I had always lived in cities. So I'd assumed I'd end up living in an international city like him. Not that there aren't hip-hoppers in Yorkshire. Especially in the late nineties when I moved here for Uni.

On one of my first big nights out in Leeds I met Seb. He was white, rocking a Starter cap and some thick-framed glasses, and it turned out he was an aspiring rapper and beatmaker. Seb approached me and a friend at a hip-hop night after several hours of us jumping on the mic and regurgitating raps that we had written at home. Seb was shy, and kind of hid behind his pineapple juice only to drop in the odd pithy comment or some deep rap trivia. Seb was into all the dope left-field hip-hop records that were emerging at the time – hip hop was being reborn. Seb's taste would influence mine. He was what they called a 'backpack rapper'. But I didn't get to hear him rap that night.

It was the following spring when I end up taking two trains and a bus to his studio – situated in the corner of his attic bedroom in his parents' house on the more rural edges of Dewsbury. His set-up is sick – an MPC, Moog synthesiser, two Technics turntables and a Neumann condenser mic he would've had to have saved a long time for. Seb plays me a number of his beats, wondering if I wanted to collab on any of them. Later I will notice that the choice of beat and subject matter of hip-hop artists in the countryside is different from their inner-city peers. Typically, the beats are jazzier and bounce more gently at mid- or downtempo. The space in the music is full of notes and textures, unlike the more harmonically stripped back and more percussively driven city-based hip hop (all apart from a tune where Seb samples the *Star Wars* 'Imperial March'). The subject matter is usually less immediate and more contemplative. Seb's verses were a good example of this – subtle but full of irony and laced with dry Yorkshire wit. But it is the reflective nature of his bars that really impresses me. I guess out of town, that's what a bit of space and the comfort of nature close by gives you. When you're not always looking at paving stones, perhaps the seasonal sways in the calendar affect you more. And when spring arrives, this new fragrance cannot help but give a sense of hopefulness.

Seb has talent and drive, but self-doubt too. He self-releases his first mixtape, puts together a hip-hop group that goes nowhere and all the while works part-time at a skater shop. He gives up rapping but continues to make beats.

Years later, I hear his life has entered another season; he has married a Leeds lass, settled in Meanwood and has signed a publishing deal. And I am so happy for him. One thing carries across hip hop, nationally and internationally – the more you get into the scene, the more you realise that, fundamentally, we are nerds waiting to come into bloom.

South Manchester. 1992. March.

When I was a kid, every so often my mum and dad would take us for walks. Sometimes I think it was with a church group. A woodland. A hill. A meadow. How is it that my dad (a South Londoner) seemed to know the names of all the plants and birds we would come across? (Cub scouts? I don't even think he went.) My inner-city Manchester education didn't give us much of nature. No more than playing conkers, the odd pine cone and the sycamore's flying helicopter seeds. All autumnal fare, not spring. (And I was kicked out of cub scouts.)

Then, family walking/rambling was something we had to do on purpose. What I mean to say is that for us, 'nature' didn't come naturally. Mainly due to the lack of access, I suppose. We got in a car and *went* somewhere. Middle-class aspirations perhaps? The same reason my parents took me to plays that none of us understood. Some notion of betterment or edification. Or perhaps deference? Either way I am grateful. Back then it was my brother's Atari ST, cartoons and the TV screen that I thought had all life and movement. But once out in an old pair of trainers in a field or woodland, the pleasures were in 3D. It was more than leisure, or even family bonding. It was a new landscape. My parents had allowed to me to be part of an image which, as a person of colour, society had often not painted me into. And I'm grateful. Even if at the time my teenage self would rather have been avoiding laser blasts on the Atari.

Calderdale. 2020. April.

Finishing my tea and putting the shoes on
Telling three kids to get a move on
Living round here is odd
We've got four supermarkets and train station
Primary school next door, access to motorways and
It's okay.

What we forget is the amount of green
Sequestered between all these.
We don't have to drive for hours. Just stumble
Around the corner to the places recommended a number
Of times by the retired couple next door.
No big mission.

Now we find what was on our doorstep
Long before the packages the delivery men bring.

Lockdown means we have new routine
So for a few months we have new routes to see.

It's a habit and it's fun. Become part of life.
So we start up the road, past cars parked on the side
Nod at a few neighbours, a half attempt at a wave, and
Turn left, past the corner shop, we're rocking pavements.
Our six-year-old tries to read a sign pointing off
Between semi-detached houses and we stop.
The boy squints: 'Public footpath.'

South Manchester. 1989. April.

After Zimbabwe, we moved back to the UK and ended up in Manchester where I spent the second half of my childhood. Here the residential, the corporate and the industrial roll out until the Greater Manchester conurbation mellows into Lancashire again.

In this city, outdoor adventure was jumping on bikes and getting lost in someone else's estate, finding an industrial wasteland, imagining ghosts in the burnt-out mini-supermarket or the stinky brook that ran through a park. Spring wasn't lost on me, but it only added a coloured tint to the former cottonopolis' civic swagger. Nature seemed far away from the concerns of the world's first modern city, a place constantly preoccupied with building upon and reinventing itself. Workhouses turned to apartments. Lives upon lives.

There was something almost sacred about grey concrete, nobility in the blackness of the old warehouse, the rough

48

reds of the man-made, shades of dirt, flesh against flaked paint on brick and smooth, dulled steel. Any little green had to squeeze between cracks, creep up the sides of drainpipes, the smallest flowers finding ledges to cling to in the brickwork of the abandoned alleyways I cycled through.

Chocolate Reflection. 2020. Spring Equinox.

Cadbury's Creme Eggs are not what they once were. The islands are shifting. In this country we don't do much for spring. The contemporary religious festival of the season is chocolate-centric. Cocoa-theism. The *de facto* sucretised secularised state. And sugar rush becomes a crash. Ostara, Germanic goddess of the dawn. Presses snooze. And Good Friday becomes sales promotion. Death and rebirth message turned zombie. The Druids had three springtime festivals, the largest being Alban Eiler, which celebrated the spring equinox (and is the festival we get the Easter egg from). There is a syncretism to it all, and adaption. An evolution of this life, these life processes, life processed, and we are left trying to unwrap the shiny foil and consume some meaning in it. As if in each subsequent generation the process and the meaning shift. And the cocoa content has been reduced. It doesn't taste the same. Sometimes I wonder if the adoption of old traditions into new ideas is like the old cassettes, each subsequent copy losing something in quality. A Tokyorkshire friend tells me that Japan has Hanami, the cherry blossom festival, celebrating the beauty and transience of flowers like a bridal party in the park. Not just

celebrating the shift out of the darkness into new spec-
trums of light and colour, but an acknowledgement of
ephemerality, fragility of life. Persephone is abducted by
Hades, caught in a cycle of catch and release. When the
next generation conflates her with older deities – silly fools
– she becomes goddess of both spring *and* death. It doesn't
taste quite the same. Even so, the repeated changes become
markers, reminders, holding a mirror to who we are. Our
renewal, our resilience, but also our creeping recklessness.
What if not only festivals or traditions change, but the very
seasons themselves are altered? If the mirror is steamed up
and murky, or if the image is cracked and incomplete; is
that a reflection of us too? The seasons are shifting. Do we
taste the same?

Terraced house, Harehills, Leeds. 2002. April.

In the basement, Cousin J works the console and adjusts
the levels. Rap-book wedged open, I sing into the mic. The
drummer/vocalist/producer and band founder nods and
smiles. Together with vocalist Shashe, at this time we are a
nu-jazz/hip-hop group called Today's Mathematics.
'Butterfly' will get me my first bit of Radio 1 airplay. My
lyrics on the verse are a happy stroll through a half-dream.
I guess my young man-self caught the themes in the air –
themes that have been associated with springtime for
millennia – new life, inspiration, change, and hope. But
even so, there is a sense in the hook that we cannot control
the elements around us – that we have to roll with what the

seasons bring us. Where do the lyrics come from? A chorus
appears:

> You cannot change the seasons
> But you can see the signs
> You may not have all the reasons
> But you can change your mind
> Keep searching, and I know you'll find
> You've been waiting for too long
> Metamorphosise
> Like a butterfly.

Monomotapa Hotel, Harare. 1984. April.

Of course we moved in April. Spring.

Only, April might be spring in Britain, but when we
stepped off the plane at Harare International we found that
in the southern hemisphere it was autumn. After the dry
season that is winter and then the summer rains – there it
is October and November when blossom begins. Spring
does a handstand.

One of my strongest memories of Harare is the towering
Monomotapa Hotel in the centre of the city. The streets
that criss-cross that part of the capital city are lined with
jacaranda trees, popping indigo confetti between official-
looking buildings. The South American trees were introduced to Zimbabwe just over a century ago.

The hotel was a curved seventies building, twenty storeys
high. There, not only could one take tea, but you could find

the full array of colour in the gardens outside. My younger self runs out to play on the trimmed grass and leaning out from the flower bed I can see the otherworldly-looking flame lilies.

The national flower comes to life in Zimbabwean spring six months after its UK counterpart. Each long, jagged petal reaches upward and curves back on itself, yellow near the base and turning red at its tips – a flame. While the petals point up vertically, the flower stamens spread out horizontally as though offering their pollen on a platter to passing trade. I learn decades later that the flame lily, *Gloriosa superba*, is actually very poisonous, containing high levels of colchicine. And although butterflies can sup the flame lily's nectar, if a dog happens to try eating the flower, the nectar can kill in around fifteen minutes. All that colour and extravagance also holds something far more unpleasant.

Calderdale. 2020. April.

Public footpath sign. And these hedges are loud.
Full of birdsong. Nests obscured from us now.
Whitethroats' or chaffinches' mating call chatter.
The tree above – I see what looks like a yellowhammer
They ask. I'm not sure. I shrug.
Wish I knew as much as my dad does.

On one side the hedges drop away to a meadow
A few scattered farmhouses, a valley, the town below.
The M62 clips the panorama's periphery
Fields are fragrant – the rush of senses hitting me.

Hectares of arable land, with woodland edges
A semicircle of spring hiding the rest of the life cycle
Where death is buried

Presenting a generous polyphony while the vista spans my
    mind
This portion of the world had been unseen from mine
Not so much a taste of Damascene blindness
But looking beyond the viewfinder
For a small sip of something sweet
Nature filling the silences

Behind the house, the traffic, the online accounts
Searching psychogeography to redefine lockdown
Being able to see the horizon
Makes one feel more expansive.
Lifts the skies. Widens the planet.
The colour saturates after months of black, grey and
    white
Creation sighs, and we oxygenate life
And as spring opens a little more, we close off the dark
As if the landscape frames not only where, but who we
    are

I spot a butterfly. And we stop.
Phone out of the pocket
Click.

It's a cabbage white.

·Scammonden Water, Kirklees. 2018. May.

Now I am the parent. Now I am the one dragging kids away from devices and out into the mud. It's only been since the children have grown a little that the residue left in my memory banks is kicking in. Myself and my wife feel the need to take the children on our outings too. And just like my dad, we make a plan. It's a mission; wellies and walking boots we forgot to clean last time, bundling them into the car and stretching seat belts across small bodies. We choose to go to Scammonden Dam. The drive takes us on a dual carriageway, down curving country roads, past the dry walls tickled by new blossoms and into a car park. Through broken treelines you can see there's a route that circles the reservoir below. As we walk, the path breaks off and runs down to a rocky beach, where someone is getting a dinghy out. There's a sailing club along the shore. The kids pick up stones and enjoy seeing the splash lap up to their wellies. I attempt to teach skimming and fail; they are just a little too young. We walk on and it's beautiful. Inevitably, about half-way around our reservoir orbit I have to carry our smallest. Three-quarters of the way round we pass a sea of bluebells attended by a green butterfly not put off by the sound of cars that is growing louder the further we walk. The north end of the horn-shaped reservoir has been cut off flat by the M62, so near the end of our walk the path turns into a tarmacked footpath running parallel with both road and water. There's a steep grassy bank to our left leading up to motorway barriers and a tall wooden fence that guards the drop into the reservoir to our right. Walking along the pathway has a sense of danger about it. The cutting rasp of heavy air turbulence made by the motorway traffic; cars, white vans, trucks and six-axle twenty-three-tonne articulated lorries pushing 70mph only a few metres away from the children's slight and clumsy bodies.

Calderdale. 2020. April.

There have always been oddities.
Only a few weeks ago
The little Morris dancer flitting
Over the farmland
Would have been hidden in bark
Or more likely the old stables we passed.
Drops in temperature
In strange years becoming stranger
Seasons become scattershot.
Oscillation a little too often
Climate change has made
The happy season treacherous.
After a milder winter deceives,
Spring receives its usual tribute
Proclamation in a blast of warmth
Which in a cold spell
Turns Brutus in the freeze.

The seasons are shifting.

Flutter. Flutter. Click.

Queensdale, Harare. 1986. May.

When we lived in Zim, I seem to remember spending most of my day barefoot and playing with our dog in between the guava trees out the front of our house. The guava crop was huge and in summer, we would sell guavas to passers-by on the road.

There was also a little smaller crop in the spring sometimes, which I'd pick when out playing. I'd sit down on the porch and enjoy the sweet pink flesh.

After the blossoms, we got ants. Flying ones. Which was always a shock to me each year; probably because I was so young. I can recall myself on barefoot patrol on the driveway – finding one insect. Then another. And another ... And then realising the whole road was covered with winged ants.

It turns out they are termites, but everyone calls them flying ants anyway. They've waited for the rains to go, and now they're out to mate and start new colonies on their nuptial flight. I remember seeing the creatures scooped up with a newspaper, or brushed into a pot or bucket, and taken home to be cooked. Ishwa – a popular dish in Zim – usually cooked up and served with the ever-present Zim staple of sadza. Spring brings food.

The flying ants drop to the earth and don't seem in a hurry to escape the local chefs gathering them up in tubs. They don't seem in a hurry at all. Too busy thinking about nuptial flights. When humankind comes along they won't know what hit them ... Turns out they taste a bit bacon-y.

Calderdale. 2020. April.

The cabbage white
Dances out of shot.
My eldest wants to see.

For butterflies
This season can be delicate
Especially as in recent decades
Spring
Has had numerous false starts
And fallen out of rhyme.

The soundtrack warping
Not so much
Echoing Vivaldi's *Spring*
As Stravinsky's effort.
It is his *Rites of Spring*
That offers us human intervention
That incurs consequence
The innocent
Dancing themselves to death.

A butterfly's life lasts
Less than a year I am told.
And if one wakes from hibernation too early
To hear the wrongs of spring
The cold
And lack of nectar

Proves too hostile
For them to last long
And end up
Whited out.

M62, the Pennines. 2008. March.

It is a Sunday. I am in between cities. Again.

The National Express coach passes Junction 21 and proceeds to slug its way up the M62 as the elevation lifts. I've managed to bag a window seat. But I'm hemmed in. Someone has sat beside me and my rucksack beneath me is pushing my knees up. I'm essentially in the foetal position on public transport. Also, the smell of eggs and onion from the sandwich of the guy next to me is depressing. My only escape is to turn my face the other way and inhale that weird musk that is left in the old coach seat synthetic fur. It has been raining in Manchester and only half an hour ago I'd had to phone a friend to confirm some information about Seb's death. I should backtrack.

Manchester. 2008. March. (The Night Before.)

The night before, after a long recording session in central Manchester, myself and the recording engineer drove through the rain to a house in Harpurhey. The house was pretty much a loose arts/social justice/faith collective. Nurses lived with musicians, who lived with asylum seekers, human rights lawyers and website designers, all mucking in and being one offbeat support network.

There was me in their lounge, uncomfortably perched on a beanbag at 1am watching the film *Brick*. It's an American high-school neo-noir movie in which the protagonist investigates the death of an ex-girlfriend. Just as the film ended – twists and all – I received a call from a music producer acquaintance. He had heard through a police friend that Seb had passed away unexpectedly. 'Is it true?' he asked. This was the first I'd heard. I don't really know the producer guy on the other end of the phone so I'm disturbed. And to be honest, it feels disrespectful. Like something privately devastating is being treated as tittle-tattle. And I don't want to disturb Seb's partner. Certainly not with a question like this. And not at 1am.

The following morning, waiting at Manchester's Chorlton Street Bus station I call up a church minister who knows Seb and his family. The minister confirms it. From that moment the day takes a surreal turn. I get on the coach, find a seat and put my rucksack under my knees.

M62, the Pennines. 2008. March.

It is with my cheek pressed up against the headrest that I notice small flecks flitting past my window. Not blossom. Not butterflies. Not flying ants. It is snow. In spring.

Home. 2020. Now.

And the seasons are in conversation
With each other
Trying to work out
What on Earth is going on.

M62, the Pennines. 2008. March.

We are reaching the highest point on any motorway in
Britain, 372 metres above sea level. Subconsciously, I don't
think I realise that the weather is strange – we're high up
– of course it's cold. We go under the Pennine Way foot-
bridge linking moors at the summit. It is only after we start
to descend and go past the Saddleworth turn-off that I realise that West Yorkshire is covered in snow. Visibility isn't
great and the driver is taking his time. We pass Scammonden
Dam. No boats on the reservoir today.

After another half an hour we split off onto the M621.
Leeds. Even as I can see the greyed-out cityscape, the trees
that watch the hard shoulder are dusted white. The wind-
screen is filled with a too-pale sky pressing down on us.
Approaching the city I can see a cemetery on one side and
sentinel Cottingley tower blocks on the other. This is usually
a welcome sight as it indicates home isn't far, but today
everything is out of joint. It feels as if spring has been arrested.

Roundabouts. Impatient traffic that isn't going anywhere.

And as we come into Leeds coach station my mobile
rings.

I look at the caller ID. It's Seb's partner. The first thing I hear is her stuttering breath trying to get the words out but she can't. So I tell her:

'I know . . . I've heard.'

I pull my rucksack out and onto my back, step off the coach, walk to the taxi rank and book a cab to her house.

It's still snowing.

Home. 2020 Now.

I press the button on the side of the phone
The gallery disappears. Locked again.

Shift in the seasons becomes a shift in psyche.
The seasons unlocked.

Spring's secret smile
A little crooked
Archetypes misremembered
Astronomers tell of orbits and rebirth
But the ground doesn't listen
To rhyme or rhythm
Seed germination fails
And hibernation wakes
Spring bulbs break
Stone fruits crumble
Migration patterns mitigated muddled

Warm welcomes turn to cold snaps
Snowdrops bow their head too low
The swift becomes the slow
The early bird catches a cold
The first cuckoo loses its place in the line
No food for the immigrant
Or those slow-movers

A shift in the seasons becomes a shifty psycho
Species killed off like jokes in poor taste
Hip-hop Morris dancer
Mother Nature's mixtape is replaced
With the shuffle function
As if Nature's caught out in the shower
Someone downstairs
Has turned on the hot tap in the kitchen sink

The turning of a door on its hinge
And someone sticks their foot in
With a bloody pamphlet
Who voted
For the seasons to deregulate themselves?

Words take on new meanings
Disordering springtime and giving it a grim instep

Walks in the woods become lonelier
Tree buds unsure whether to peep

When the skies are so volatile
Eden is interrupted again
Primary tones become discoloured
Seasons shift

And the butterfly
In search of nectar
Perches
A little too long
Crystallised
In hoarfrost

Click.

SUMMER

Severn Beach

Michael Malay

A few years ago, during a dry period of life, when I felt
severed from the places I knew as home, I began going to a
place called Severn Beach. It's a village ten miles north of
Bristol, at the end of the local train line. At first I went
every few months, but it wasn't long before I began visiting
every fortnight and then every week.

The place is a little hard to explain. Had you come a
hundred years ago, you would have found hotels and tea
gardens, funfairs and donkey rides, as well as an outdoor
swimming pool called The Blue Lagoon. Every summer,
tourists visited in their thousands, to take in the sea air by
the estuary or drink tea shipped in from Ceylon and India.
But today an air of neglect hangs over the place. The hotels
and tea gardens disappeared in the 1970s, the public pool
was demolished in the '80s, and the last pub closed in 2002.
Arriving at the train station, you'll find the flowerbeds left
untended and the platform littered with broken glass, beer
cans and crisp packets. A clairvoyant practises her trade near
the village centre, offering to read your spirit worlds, and
just over a mile away, beyond a set of fields, are the distribution centres for Tesco, Next and B&M.

Still, it's a quietly extraordinary place, and now, whenever I'm away for too long, I find myself growing grim about the mouth, deprived of something good and free.

When you leave the station you'll find a small ramp at the end of the street. Climb it. This is the sea wall of Severn Beach, and as you mount it you're often scoured by wind, which sweeps past in short manic bursts or long relentless squalls. You are at one of the edges of England, meeting the winds as they arrive from the Atlantic, and before you is the rocky, muddy, salty, light-filled world of the Severn Estuary. Big sky, big water. Miles of mud.

The climb is always worth the view, even in freezing winter winds, for nothing stays the same at Severn Beach. The birds are always coming and going, the mudflats emerging or receding, and the tides retrieving something new, from the Anthropocene detritus of fridges, plastic helmets and galvanised buckets, to the gifts of mermaid's purses, polished driftwood and ravelled seagrass. It's a reliably smelly place – the rotting seaweed and sulphurous mud get right up your nose – but it's also full of glorious sleights of hand. When the sun burnishes the water with the right sheen – the sheen of hammered gold, or of mackerel shoals turning beneath the sun – the estuary can look strangely insubstantial, less estuary than a floating plane of light. Then it seems to levitate above the seafloor, as if, at this time of light-dazzle, water were exempt from the laws governing mass. The effect is particularly strong in the summer, when heat and light thicken the air, but I've also seen the same effect on bright winter days. Always, though, the estuary's pong brings you back to earth, rubbing salt and mud into your visions of another world.

I didn't like it at first. Many years ago, when I first arrived in Britain, I visited Severn Beach on a whim, curious to see what lay at the end of the local train line. I came on a day of wind and rain and remember feeling disappointed by what I saw: mile upon mile of mudflats, a desolate coast, and the estuary's rocky channels exposed by the ebbing of the tide. To the south was the port of Avonmouth, a series of cranes and squat buildings, while to the north were the imposing girders and towers of one of the Severn bridges, with its constant heave of traffic. There was no place to swim, no sand to sift through your fingers, and nothing that you could recognise as 'beach'. Or, rather, nothing I could recognise as beach. As a boy growing up in Indonesia, beaches meant the hot sands of Parangtritis, Kuta or Sambolo, and later, when my family moved to Queensland, Australia, it meant the beaches of Surfers Paradise, South Stradbroke and Rainbow Bay. And although I had tempered my expectations upon visiting Severn Beach, I still wasn't prepared for the sight of so much mud. I don't think I stayed for very long.

But if I didn't care for this estuary when I first arrived, I now feel drawn to it. I like to see what happens here: the birds banking in the freedom of the air, the tides generating deep water-folds by the pylons of the bridge, and the island of Flat Holm glowing in late afternoon sun, a bar of gold laid across the estuary. Increasingly, I have also been coming for what I cannot see. Every spring, juvenile eels arrive here in their millions from the Atlantic Ocean and, every autumn, adult eels depart in their thousands, leaving their river dwellings for the Sargasso Sea. And in between these comings and goings are certain yellow eels who, having migrated here many years ago, and being content to go no further upstream, made this estuary their home. Somehow, despite the churn of forces passing through this place — billions of litres of water, carrying millions of tonnes of silt — the eels had found a way of staying put. They would be here right now, on the other side of the seawall, muscled cables lengthening in the dark.

'There are tides in the body', Virginia Woolf wrote, secret urgings and hidden gravitational forces. Not all of them make sense. Walking along Severn Beach, I some-times wonder at the pull this place has on me, and how different things were when I first stood here. That younger self was homesick for the places he had left behind, for known customs and manners, but he was also excited by this place called England, by the world at his nose. Still, he thought of himself as a visitor, living here on borrowed time. So how odd to be drawn here week after week, walking along the seawall as oystercatchers wheel above the estuary; and how strange to be combing the shingle beach for bits of driftwood, or skipping rocks across the water, not as a boy in Indonesia, or a teenager in Australia, but as a grown man on the shores of the Severn. I have come to know this place over the years, perhaps even to love it, although 'love' may not be the right word, for the estuary is neither a sentimental nor a forgiving place. 'You have to understand it inside out,' my friend Jessie once told me, 'or you'll be in trouble'. Having spent years sailing around the coasts of Britain and Ireland, she tells me that the estuary, with its formidable currents and tides, its concealed sandbars and rocky islands, is one of the most dangerous places she's experienced. But that's also part of the attraction. Though we come to its edges, to wonder at the bright flowing unstillness of it all, the estuary is its own place, with its own wild mind, and has no regard for what we think.

Eels are tiny when they are born, no bigger than a grain of rice, and completely transparent. If you looked at them closely, you would see into the world. But as they grow older they begin to absorb light, to bend and to capture it. Their skins darken, their bodies lengthen, and their translucency is replaced by a murky brown. Streaks of yellow run down their flanks, like bars of muddy gold, and their eyes grow more pronounced. The grain of rice has become a yellow eel. But the transformations only continue, change following change. As they grow older, their yellow flanks darken, shade into umber, until, reaching full maturity, they take on the colours of a starry midnight. A slick, glossy black covers their top half, while their underbellies take on a silvery sheen. Glints of brown and green cover their back like flecks of mica. The yellow eel has become a silver eel.

European eels are born in the Sargasso Sea, where they emerge from unknown depths – unknown because, despite many attempts, no one has ever seen them mate in the wild. Rising as eggs on the water column, they tumble out of tiny yolk sacs, and during these first months they do not look like eels so much as willow leaves, with their flared-out bodies tapering to a fine point. (Newborn eels are known as *leptocephali*, meaning 'slim head'.) At first, these willow leaves are unable to swim, and so they float on the great ocean roads of the Gulf Stream and North Atlantic Drift. These are the same currents that carried their ancestors east and that allow them to travel extraordinary distances: eels entering the coastal waters of Ireland and Britain will have travelled four thousand miles, while those that travel to Latvia, Estonia and Iceland will have gone even further, some as far as five thousand miles.

Later in life, some of these eels will continue travelling, happy to drift like houseboats. Most, however, will become faithful to a particular place. After reaching home ground – it could be an estuary, river, stream, lake, pond or ditch – they will create little burrows in the earth, by clearing away mud with their powerful snouts. And they will stay there for years, resting in the daytime and hunting at night.

And then, many years later, the long journey home ... On autumn nights, when the moon is in its last quarter, and after rain has swollen the rivers, adult eels will quietly leave their mud-holes, turn their noses west, and swim for the

Sargasso. It's a place they hardly know, having left it when they were only one or two weeks old, yet it's a seascape written into their bodies, and to which they return with fateful precision. Beginning its life as a wayfarer, the eel ends its life as one too, and perhaps it always knew this moment would come: this quiet sea-journey, this long swim home.

What might that be like, to feel the call of home from four thousand miles away? Is it a hunger? An ache? Or something stronger?

A flock of dunlin fly across the estuary, white bellies flashing against the sun, and in the distance I can see dozens of Canada geese, a circle of pagans on the saltmarsh. I continue along the estuary, towards the headwaters of the Severn, and when I stop to inspect a ditch next to a muddy field – a shallow trench shimmering with yesterday's rain – I realise that I am happy. For it is summer in England, the days have been long and roomy, and I woke up knowing that I could walk for many hours into the day's extended light, and then, if I wished, on into the evening, always deeper into the blueness. The length of these summer days was still a novelty. In Indonesia, where I lived until I was ten years old, the nights would come on swiftly – when the sun set, you'd be in the dark – and it was much the same in Australia, where I lived until I was twenty. But in England the hills would hold the light for hours, as though the sun had become stuck during its descent – wedged just below the horizon and yet close enough to light everything up: the valleys, the skies, the paths.

I reach the middle of the saltmarsh, shin-deep in the churned-up path. By the ponds, a swan lifts the white block of itself into the air, before settling again onto the water, and along the estuary are thousands of birds, beaks down, looking for food in the mud. From where I stand, and as the sun strikes the shoreline, it seems as though they are walking on vast iridescent sheets, a wet golden fire. Some of the estuary's birds are year-long residents, and there's a good chance of seeing them most days: kestrels, little egrets, the Canada geese. Others visit for the winter before heading north again in the spring: teal, wigeon, shelduck. Still others are just passing through for a couple of days. But they come in such numbers! – hundreds of dunlin and oystercatcher, lapwing and redshank, knot and ringed plover, all drawn here to the open-air buffet of the Severn Estuary. When they've had their fill, they rise into the air again, a whir of restlessness.

Powerful winds swirl through the estuary, creating hollows and wavelets in the water. Then a stronger gust follows, half spinning me on my heels, and as my head is turned from estuary to saltmarsh I'm able to follow the wind's surging run across the fields, which announces itself in flattened grass, flailing scrub and the sudden blurring of trees. I laugh, surprised by its strength, and for a moment, as more gusts batter the saltmarsh, the familiar landmarks of Severn Beach seem to fall away, so that, instead of the estuary's usual colours and landmarks, what I see are wavering lines and flexing forces, a grid of unstable energies of which the wind and the tides and the birds were only a part. The moment passes, the winds stop, but now the estuary seems a little brighter, as if light had been poured onto the water from above, or had risen up from the mud itself.

I walk on, towards the settlement of Aust, where a ferry once carried passengers to Beachley.

Eels are tenacious creatures. In *A History of British Fishes* (1836), William Yarrell describes an experiment in which eels were buried in snow, left to freeze over, and later transferred to a bucket, whereupon they thawed and 'soon perfectly recovered'. They are also known to survive to an astonishing age. In parts of northern Europe, where eels were sometimes kept in wells (their voracious appetites made them useful as filter-feeders), one such creature, the so-called Brantevik Eel of Sweden, lived for 155 years.

So they know something about endurance.

They are also canny creatures. Today, European rivers are blocked by many obstructions: weirs, dams, sluice gates. After four thousand miles of open ocean, then, the eels are suddenly confronted by walls. Environmentalists have counted more than 600,000 such barriers in Europe, although the real number is likely to exceed one million.

Still, the creatures press on. They can squeeze through the slightest cracks in our infrastructure and have a wonderful ability to climb up tidal gates, dams and water-falls. Sometimes, you will see them clambering over each other as they form dense mats on the surface of a wall, a process known in America as 'roping up'. They will not be deterred. They are driven by an instinct stronger than hope.

Eels are also devoted citizens of place. Not many people know this. We think of them as migrants and wayfarers, but in fact they are lovers of continuity. For most of their life, they stay close to their home burrows, making only modest journeys during the course of a hunting trip. There are exceptions. Some eels, like some humans, are drifters, always curious about the next bend upriver. Other eels drift with the seasons, retreating to warmer bodies of water between November and March, when their usual dwellings become too cold, before reappearing in the spring, like holidaymak-ers returning from abroad. For the most part, though, the view laid down by Friedrich-Wilhelm Tesch, one of the recognised authorities on eels, remains broadly true. Despite its extraordinary capacity for travel, the eel 'maintains a very restricted home range, even if broad expanses of water are open in all directions'.

This attachment to home does not always make sense. In 1968, 350 yellow eels were captured in Heligoland, a small archipelago in the North Sea. The eels were marked, taken many miles from their home territory, and then released. A few months later, when scientists returned to the archi-pelago, they found that dozens of the eels had returned to the same place they had been discovered, an area measuring 3 x 4 kilometres. Similar experiments were replicated elsewhere – on the North Friesland island of Föhr, and near the village of Den Oever, in Holland – and yielded comparable results. The eel is possessed of an unusual 'homing ability', Tesch concludes of these studies, one which has 'yet to be seen so clearly in any other species of fish, and which is reminiscent of the qualities shown by homing pigeons'.

How might that feel, to be displaced and still know your way back? And for home to be printed so delicately on your body, or stamped so forcefully onto your mind, that to be away from it is a kind of malady?

'There is something libidinous' to the feeling of home-sickness, Jan Morris writes, as though missing home were a whole-body ache, at once dark and painful and sweet.

I am thinking of the eels of Heligoland now, as I pick my way across the muddy saltmarsh. A few weeks ago, a man on the radio was talking about 'Anywheres' and 'Somewheres', and the simplicity of his analysis has been bothering me all month. If you are one of the 'Anywheres', he had explained, then you are part of that restless tribe of the metropolitan middle class, whose identities are portable because not attached to certain places or communities; but if you are a 'Somewhere', your identity is deeply rooted in tradition, community, landscape. You belong to a particular world, and it belongs to you. In reality, he conceded, things were a little more complicated – the categories were not watertight. Nevertheless, he had pressed on with his theme. The Somewheres are a place-bound people who tend to be more conservative in their politics; the Anywheres, more likely to be liberally progressive, are as happy in one city as they are in the next.

I know I am simplifying the man's argument. I'm sure his thinking is more nuanced than I have made out. But what has been troubling me is how cleanly he was willing to draw his lines. *For the sake of analysis* – yes, I understand. And yet his ideas seemed to recapitulate a way of thinking that itself seemed part of the problem – a division of the country into the rootless and the rooted, and into those who belonged and those who were passing through. But where do eels fit into this picture? Travellers from the faraway, they are nevertheless attached to particular places – a stretch of river, a sweep of estuary, an underwater shelf in the North Sea. They are both wayfarers and locals, migrants and natives, and so transcend the binaries we too often pit against each other. For you might be a traveller with many miles under your belt and still know what it means to love a place: the unchanging view, the rounded horizon. Or you might live deeply within your own bounds and still be open to the ongoingness of change. I think of my Indonesian grandparents, eyeing up my father, and wondering why, of all the good Muslim men in Java, my mother settled for a Catholic farm boy from Illinois. My grandparents had never left Indonesia before – in fact, the furthest they ever travelled was to Semarang, seventy miles north of their city of Yogyakarta – but they opened their house to him anyway, gave him food and drink. A year later, my father converted to Islam, married my mother, and put down roots in Jakarta, where he would raise a family of four. I have a picture of them from their wedding day: Dad is wearing a Javanese wedding costume, including a blangkon, a traditional Javanese hat.

A flock of geese lift up from the saltmarsh, charging the air with their wings and loud cries. They rise into the light, the amazing light at Severn Beach, which says to you: *stop thinking and watch this show I'm putting on.* But my head is whirring, a thought-flock of words, and I can't step out of my mind, which is where I know the estuary begins. I am still thinking about the eels of Heligoland, but I see now that I am simplifying matters, and that things are much more complex than I have made out. In the imaginary debates I was conducting in my head, eels were models of cosmopolitan rootedness. With their sleek heads and anguine bodies, they rhymed with the flowing environments in which they lived, but they also experienced the world from their burrows – stable centres in the midst of flux. And I suppose that's how I also saw Severn Beach, a shifting territory where water meets land, river meets sea, freshwater meets saltwater, as well as a place of continuity, rhythm, repetition. Each tide was incorrigibly new; each tide also continued an ancient song.

And yet, only four miles along the estuary, at the port of Avonmouth, another series of transformations constantly takes place, the flow of goods and commodities, capital and wealth. Every year, thousands of tonnes of jet fuel arrive here from the Middle East, fuel that is sent on to Heathrow and Gatwick via underground pipes. And it is where other ships appear carrying cargo of all kinds: coal from Australia, animal feed from Argentina and Brazil, metals from South Africa, as well as British MGs made in China. Ecologically and culturally, there is nowhere else like the Severn Estuary, but from another perspective, that of capital, it is simply a node in an international network, one of many links in a global supply chain. In my mind, the eels and the estuary were ambassadors of flow, and yet flow can also mean liquidity – the conversion of assets into cash, the melting of once-solid things (coherent traditions, patterns of life), and the dream of frictionless capital mobility. Is there a way of separating the strands, so that one can differentiate flow from liquidity, transformation from displacement? Or are they too tangled up? I think again of my father, an employee of an Australian mining company based in Jakarta. He left America out of a sense of adventure, but his presence in Indonesia was also part of a larger transformation, one in which the country's resources were literally extracted by multinational corporations, from the Freeport gold mine in West Papua to the Chevron oil fields in central Sumatra. The developments brought wealth to the country – new jobs, new highways, new shopping malls – but mostly the riches flowed outwards, to companies and stockholders in the global North, or into the bank accounts of corrupt Indonesian politicians.

More winds buffet the estuary, stirring the water and waking the land, and at the edge of the saltmarsh I can see a kestrel flickering above its square of grass. By now I have reached the old ferry terminal at Aust, where the *Severn King* and *Severn Queen* once transported passengers to Beachley, on the estuary's other shore. In 1966, one of those travellers was Bob Dylan. The day before, he had played a show in Bristol, and later that night would be standing on a stage in Cardiff, accompanied by four tonnes of amplification. A year after his crossing, the ferry terminal would be decommissioned, made obsolete by the completion of the Severn Bridge. The pier and the ferry building are still there, but they are rotting into the mud now, and in a few decades they'll have been claimed by the estuary.

I think of the people I saw on the train that morning, some of whom I now know by sight. There were the teachers, office workers and shop assistants who would alight at Montpelier, the high-school students who would bustle off at Redland, and the university lecturers, graduate students and young professionals who would step off at Clifton Down. Afterwards, the train would mostly empty out, and there would usually be one kind of passenger left: migrant workers – men who have taken low-paying jobs at Avonmouth docks, or at the many distribution centres clustered around the port. They are from all over the world – India, Spain, Poland, Hungary – and although we take the same train, we are bound for different places. They go to work for £10 an hour to stack shelves or to unload cargo into a warehouse, whereas my stop is Clifton, near the university where I worked, or Severn Beach, where I would go to visit the estuary. The train stops are only separated by a few miles, but it is a long journey.

Maersk, Hapag-Lloyd, CMA CGM: the names of the containers on the cargo ships entering Avonmouth. The boats also come from all over the world – Liberia, Russia, Gibraltar – and sometimes, after a trip to Severn Beach, I would log onto a website at home, to see what boats had visited Avonmouth that day: the *Agia Eleni*, a bulk carrier registered to the Marshall Islands, the *Waaldijk*, a cargo ship from the Netherlands, and *Maris*, a container ship from Cyprus. The economic forces propelling these ships have transfigured the world, connecting Manila with Monaco, Paris with Phnom Pen, but as much as they brought places together, they have partly undermined them too. The conditions of the migrant workers at Avonmouth docks are, increasingly, the same conditions of the 'Somewheres' living under austerity Britain: stagnant wages, rising rents, precarious work, and a feeling of being decentred from your own community, your own life. I think of Dylan crossing the estuary in the spring of 1966. Far from home. Riding the tides of the Severn. A rolling stone, like so many of us now. A traveller on a ship somewhere between England and Wales.

It was the eels that helped me to see the shipping containers. To reach Severn Beach, you have to stop at Avonmouth, and this means passing through a rusting hinterland of industrial architecture: metal tanks, distribution warehouses, gantries and derricks. And it was this weekly experience of seeing Avonmouth – all that evidence of our trading and

manufacturing, our buying and selling – that got me thinking about flow and liquidity, and about the different
processes that were happening in this one place. Emissaries
of flow, eels effortlessly cross all sorts of geographical and
national borders; but so do the cargo ships. Two very different processes – the arrival of jet fuel from Kuwait, and the
arrival of elvers from the Sargasso – occur in the same environment. But can they be separated, I wondered? Can you
have the meeting of cultures without the homogenising
effects of capital, and can you have the renewal of the ordi-
nary without the destruction of the old? I wasn't sure, and
I felt lost even thinking about it, bewildered by the vastness
of that question.

I should probably turn back now, the afternoon is beginning to fade, but I'm seized by the urge to keep going, to
walk on and on into the summer. Now Aust Warth is
behind me, and I'm climbing a hill known as Potato Tump,
just past the Severn Bridge. Three miles to the southwest, I
can see the second bridge that was constructed over the
estuary in 1996, and beyond that, just about visible, is the
island of Flat Holm, first named by the Vikings more than
a thousand years ago. They brought other names to this part
of the British Isles, some of which are still in use – Anglesey,
Skerries, Milford Haven – and although 'holm' was their
word for a small island, every time I hear it I think of
'home'. What was it like, that moment of arrival, the enigma
of seeing a new world? Sometimes I wonder at those
Vikings, so far from their home fields, setting their eyes
upon Steep Holm and Flat Holm. Were they content with

their longboat lives, or were they thinking of the places they left behind, or perhaps it was both?

The distant cry of oystercatchers, the tide rushing in, and now warm light running across the estuary, making the water shimmer. Earlier that day, I had received a text from my mother in Yogyakarta, which read: 'about to get ready for breaking puasa'. And maybe it was this that had got me thinking of holm and home, for today was the end of Ramadan, and 'puasa', which meant fasting, was at an end. That evening, a feast would be laid out on the tables of my mother's house, where uncles, aunts and cousins would gather to eat, a scene that would be replicated in house-holds all over the country. 'Pulang kampung', people would have been saying to each other before the celebrations began, as they prepared to travel to their family homes. 'To return to one's home village', 'to go back home'.

Another flock edges into vision, this time a cloud of redshank. They fly in the softness of afternoon light, along-side other migrant birds who have come from southern Europe and Africa, all drawn to the Severn's worm-rich muds. How do they find their way here, to these saltmarshes, to this estuary? Perhaps they feel home as a rightness in their bodies, and perhaps that feeling of rightness is not something they know in advance but something that has to be discovered as they move towards it. Always, for the first time, the birds have to remember what they do not know: that *here* is body-feeling-right while *there* is something-missing, and that, once they are *here* again, the longing in their bodies would subside, at least for the moment. The redshank-cloud returns to earth – a hundred feet clicking into place – and then, as if in obedience to a hidden signal, a group of oystercatchers lift themselves up and flock above the waters.

I loved seeing these birds. They came and went, topped the place up and emptied it out, so that watching them was like observing a quicker version of the tides. Sometimes they swung far out over the estuary, where they dwindled into specks or disappeared altogether, but mostly they moved up and down the shoreline, tumbling softly in the air. Not all would come back. Occasionally, after getting up from the ground, some birds would wing themselves over the water and keep on going. As you watched them fly, you could feel your own body light up with an electric pulse that was hard to name, the pull of your own life's adventure.

The day is slipping away now; it's time to turn back. That night, I would be meeting some friends for a late dinner in Easton, a suburb in Bristol. 'An empty stomach', a friend had texted, when I asked what I should bring, 'we're cooking a big pie!' She hadn't known I would be thinking that day of home, of pulang kampung, and of the feast that would be laid on at my mother's house.

I walk back to Severn Beach, along the muddy saltmarsh from where I have come, and give the estuary one last look before boarding the train. Then I find a seat in a middle carriage, put my earphones in, and play an album I've been listening to for months now, the songs repeated so often they have become part of my brain. And as Bowie sings about the colour blue, the last of the summer light dissolves over Avonmouth, so that the window, losing the image of the world, gains the reflection of the carriage: two men drinking beer at a table, a woman reading a book. A luminous train at the edge of England.

Walk. Don't Walk

Jay Griffiths

With pockets full of apples, a rucksack and a pair of boots, this is my dream. To set out at lark rise with the rising sun, happy-go-lucky as if summer lasts forever and all the world will always be gorgeous with sunshine. Out! Onwards! Walk till evening, then sleep under the stars and in the morning, again, on, on in the timeless vagabondage of glee and freedom.

I want to set out like this every midsummer morning, with a flute or a fiddle and a flask of wine, a sketchbook, a copy of the *Rubaiyat of Omar Khayyam* and a caravanserai of fellow travellers in my heart.

'I felt it was for this I had come: to wake at dawn on a hillside and look out on a world for which I had no words, to start at the beginning, speechless and without plan, in a place that still had no memories for me', as Laurie Lee wrote in *As I Walked Out One Midsummer Morning*.

Walk your path right into tomorrow because the Way will never run out, endlessly opening to elsewhere. Such is the call heard by Isabelle Eberhardt, writing: 'A nomad I was even when I was very small and would stare at the road, that spellbinding white road headed straight for the unknown ... and I shall stay a nomad all my life, in love with changing horizons, unexplored, far-away places ...'

This is how the stale patina of routine is banished. Everything shines with newness and I'm all whiskers and nose, delightfully drunk on dawn as Time and the Way rhyme in their invitation to set out on the grand adventure of your life and – full tilt, streaming ribbons, hurling yourself into it all – the only way to go is to play Pied Piper to your own youthful self.

I am beckoned by the very word 'bridleway' and every footpath tempts my feet as it tickles the map. The network of public rights of way covers 140,000 miles in England and Wales plus 9,300 miles in Scotland. It is one of the UK's greatest cultural achievements, rare and precious. I clutch the passport that grants me my ability to roam: an Ordnance Survey map, at the scale of 1:25,000. The path planned on the map and found on the land sets off a peal of bells. This is pure happiness. As a teenager, I pictured Cornwall as a wall of golden-yellow corn; I could hear the warmth in the name 'Devon' and felt that Somerset – a summer settlement – was full of sun. With an OS map and a compass I could make it mine.

I need to say, though, that I'm not as confident at orienteering as I would like to be. My brothers, as Sea Scouts, were taught all this from a young age. I tried, encouraged by my mother, to be allowed to join these scouts but the leader shot me down: 'You can't. You're a girl.' Recently rereading Tove Jansson's *Summer Book*, I was delighted that it was 'because of Grandmother' that girls were allowed to be Scouts in Finland. But I wasn't, and so to my list of setting out with a flute, a flask and a sketchbook, I added one more: to be a *boy* is to be able to properly drink in the wine of summer, to respond to the call and to travel, to venture in seasonal migration, a transhumance of delight.

Taking a flitting tent, a bivouac or hammock, I wanted to stretch my wings and become bird, part of that migratory instinct so widely felt in humans, magnetised to flight, for holidays, caravans, getaways, drawn to islands large and small, the Maldives, Martinique, the Seychelles and the very idea of archipelagos. In anticipation of migration, we become like birds, gathering, chittering with the swallows, feeling the wind in our feathers, soaring within. 'Mountains pulled and pushed,' writes Robyn Davidson in *Tracks*, 'wind roared down chasms. I followed eagles suspended from cloud horizons. I wanted to fly in the unlimited blue of the morning.'

Birds are literally magnetised, many having magnetite in their beaks, a mineral that can work like a compass, aligning the bird to the earth's magnetic field. Birds prepare in different ways: a sandpiper, for instance, can shrink its organs so it can better undertake the journey. As the days get longer and warmer, birds such as the swallow get nervy and twitchy. *Zugunruhe* is the word for this: the restlessness that birds feel at the tug of the migratory instinct. Their wings flutter: they sleep less. If a robin is caged, even with no sight of the outdoors, it will hurl itself northwards, slamming itself against glass walls, and somehow always, always knowing true north.

And humans? Is the urge innate? Perhaps so. There is a gene, DRD4, that helps control dopamine, associated with learning and reward. That gene has a variant, DRD4-7R, that is carried by about 20 per cent of humans and that variant is repeatedly linked to curiosity and restlessness, making people more likely to take risks and to explore, be it places or ideas, embracing movement, novelty, change and adventure. Moreover, as *National Geographic* reports, several studies link that 7R variant to human migration: it is found more often in migratory cultures than in settled ones. The variant doesn't exactly make someone adventurous but, acting with other genetic factors and certain environmental backgrounds, can influence the urge.

However it comes about, I know I feel my own *Zugunruhe* in early summer. I wake earlier, rise earlier, each sunrise strengthening me in the rising year, a sense of rising wind lifting my wings, and often I want to go up to the north, to the top of the map, up to the sky – and to Skye and the islands.

I used to go there every summer when I was younger. It was a long drive, passing near to Gavin Maxwell's house and the setting for *Ring of Bright Water*. It involved a ferry to the Isle of Skye, then more road, another ferry to a further island, Raasay, and another drive to the point where the road ends. And then a long walk down to the sea's edge and there it was: a tiny, low-lying island, barely half a mile across, shaped like a shield and set in its own ring of bright water. You could reach that third island only by crossing a tidal causeway when the tide was out.

It was an island of cotton-grass and lochs and oyster-catchers. I saw the Northern Lights there, faintly shimmering green, and once I lay for hours on a low cliff watching sea otters circling each other, nose to tail, in the perpetual motion of play. It was uninhabited by humans, enchanted and beloved. It was also very, very damp. A friend of mine came with me once, and on arrival took a deep and satisfied breath then pronounced: 'Any fool can appreciate a mountain, but it takes a man of genuine discernment to appreciate a bog.'

The first time I went there, I saw with manifest delight that this tiny island had an island-child of its own, just a few feet across and a couple of feet high. Islands accord so well with summer: Tove Jansson's *Summer Book* is set on another small and beloved island in the Gulf of Finland; the Isle of Avalon, island of apples, has always had a summer feel to me.

When I was an adolescent, I drew an island and filled it with all the things I loved: swings and slides and see-saws and merry-go-rounds and a lake and a mountain and paths, a camping place with a little tent on the western shore, a wishing tree with apples and flowers and a fancy-dress costume, and a little path that led to a thatched cottage with roses in the garden. There were streams with interesting footbridges and trees to climb. In a harbour on the eastern side, I'd drawn a little sailing boat which could charter a course to the mainland. I had marked the harbour with an arrow pointing away from the island to the main-land, and by the arrow, a note that said 'People'. There was an island-off-the-island, with a trampoline, a hopscotch game, a table-tennis table and a croquet lawn. And then there was another tiny island with a shelter and views to everywhere. I had called it 'Liber Isle'. I was learning Latin at the time, and this was my Isle of Books, so I could be happily isolated there whenever I liked and, through books, be able to see far horizons. Although I didn't intend a pun at the time, the word 'liber' also means 'free': the freedom of the endless days of summer to read endlessly. And a book itself is an island of sorts; in the stormy sea of 'real' life, a book is an island refuge, a good place to be happily shipwrecked.

On my paper island, it was always summer. It was my place of achieved destination, of safety and repletion. Everything was in perfect balance, happiness in stasis, an emotional solstice of summation and completion. And what is midsummer but the idyllic island in the sea of the year? The set-apart time, the perfect circlet, as the sun is the perfect golden island in its sea of blue sky.

In summer, everything melts. People melt into each other's arms in the caress of the sun, delirious, cidery and warm, ah Rosie, ah Laurie. Winter is unforgiving with its cold shoulders and chilly responses, but summer melts resentments into benediction. All the metal months, the earth-hard-as-iron seasons, are thawed then warmed. Everything sharp is softened: the thorn gives way to the rose, the silky and soft and tender things, love-in-a-mist, butterflies, a world of petal not metal.

I melt into all the characters of my childhood books. I am Heidi, walking up a mountain, nearer and nearer the sun, intoxicated by the smell of cut grass and hay, light-stepping as she takes off her heavy clothes, the restrictive grumpy clothes of the grown-up world, and steps barefoot in a petticoat, lighthearted and free. But I never dressed in petticoats. As a girl, I was a boy, more Tom Sawyer than Heidi, in shorts and a grubby T-shirt, sand-scuffed and tanned. *Find a boat!* A rowing boat to row around the island all day. *Borrow one! Don't ask: they might say no.* Make an oar from any old plank. No one will know. *It was the sun's fault, honest. Summer dared me to do it.*

I am so exultantly drunk on summer itself that I have melted, saturated, steeped and soaked, I am being drunk by summer in turn. I melt into everything I see. A turtle, so floating, so free. A hot cat too sun-lazy to move a paw until September.

Herman Melville, in a letter to Nathaniel Hawthorne, wrote: 'You must often have felt it, lying on the grass on a warm summer's day. Your legs seem to send out shoots into the earth. Your hair feels like leaves upon your head. This is the *all* feeling.'

Ringing with optimism, I hear the season, the rising arpeggio in A major played by an old accordionist, wick as a cricket with his sun-smoked hands and accompanied by cicadas. Up, up to the height of the year. The largesse of the season in a sunflower clambering upward, sheaves of corn growing taller by the hour, the berries ripening and flowers bursting: there will be food in the hedges and no need for payment, as summer is sumptuous in generosity.

'In summer, the song sings itself,' wrote William Carlos Williams. Summer is honeysuckled and cannot be sinister. Foxgloves for a child's fingertips, lavender and marigold. Smelling the sweet fermentation of silage makes me dizzy with delight. The heliotropes are in love with the sun, turning at every moment, sun seeking with every petal, and the daisy, the 'day's eye', opens and closes with the dawn and dusk, holding in itself a tiny model of the golden sun with its paler rays. Sweet pea tendrils sway and bend and reach in curlicues for the upward swing of the thing. The hedgerows stretch towards me: 'The nectarine and curious peach/Into my hands themselves do reach' as Andrew Marvell wrote. Everything wants to reach out and touch you, wasps, apples, sticky-grass, brambles: everything stretches to its full extent. I want that too. Heart flung wide open, into the blue-gold, rays stretching wide as St Francis's arms, outstretched in joy for Brother Sun. Everything stretches into everything else, yearning, reaching, wanting; light into more light, today into tomorrow, growing, opening into the rising sky.

It is light all the time.

It is time all the light.

Skyfuls of sun, daylight at midnight and nothing benighted.

The plants count the hours of light and measure the temperature in order to time their flowering in the sweet and complex clock of the natural world, keeping its rhythm, in time with itself, the unconquerable promise of light and life with time and truth as if, no matter how harsh the winter has been and no matter how capricious the spring, the world agrees with Albert Camus: 'In the midst of winter, I found there was, within me, an invincible summer.'

And then the sun is itself at full stretch, the height of its light. In the zenith – at the solstice – the great *yes* of midsummer in the uttermost reach of the year, perfect balance in perfect harmony. After its risings and before its fallings. After it has forgotten spring and before it will hint of autumn. After the crescendo of spring with brightening days and birdsong louder and earlier, and before autumn's decrescendo, its lowering skies and the birds quieter and later. Between. In the centre of the year there is this now, all now, and how it shines. Solstice is an island in time, a tidal island between spring's tide inwards and upwards and autumn's tide outwards and downwards.

The sweetest rendition of the summer solstice I've ever read is in *The Wind in the Willows*. Mole and Rat are awake rowing the river, looking for little Portly, the young otter. Set on Midsummer Night, that chapter is at the mid-point, the heart of the year. And the chapter is right in the middle of the book, and is the soul of the story. Among the shaded green banks and the cool dark water, with the sound of the wind in the osiers, and when everything is made magical by the soft and endless light, they come to an island in the middle of the river. This is the core place, the centre in space as in time. There they find the little otter. But more: there, too, they find the core magic, the central divinity of the book, for the otter is being guarded by Pan himself, god of nature. His music – 'simple, passionate, perfect' – is The Song at the absolute heart of it all. It is the dream-state where the deepest truth is told.

I read that chapter aloud once to my then eight-year-old god-daughter, sharing the voices with her mother who had made a circle of petals on the grass, so the three of us could sit inside the ring of bright flowers: a solstice ceremony as perfect as it was simple.

No night. No bedtime. Summer evaporated the rules. It was our own Midsummer Night's Dream, a realm of easy magic and gentle charm, a night when all was well and there was nothing more concerning than the love potion that Puck makes from the wild pansy, or love-in-idleness.

A cloud comes over the sun, in my mind. How come my own midsummer dream is so simple and yet so impossible? For right at the apex of the year, the moment to stretch your wings, set out for sheer freedom, I am grounded. Caged.

My freedom comes from my kit. My beloved Trangia, that lightweight and reliable stove. Waterproof matches. My tent, waterproof in any storm. My sleeping bag that will keep me cosy down to minus twenty. My top-of-the-range Therm-a-Rest. My Swiss Army penknife.

My unfreedom comes from my gender. I am frightened of being alone on the dusty lanes and paths specifically because I am scared of being sexually assaulted by a man.

No amount of experience of the vast majority of good-hearted men-o'-th'-woods can ever quell the fear. When I want to get right inside summer like a seed in a sunflower, I find there is a grubby Perspex shield between me and the full experience I crave. I can see it — the bridleway, the campfire, the tavern — but I cannot inhabit it as I wish. I know it is my right, as simple and absolute as the sun's right to rise. But it is disallowed.

No law forbids me. But it doesn't have to. Experience censors women's freedom. The result is I feel suffocated, denied the precise air I need. I am constricted. I have been planted not out in the commons but in a pot where my roots cannot spread properly. I have been bonsaied. And I hate it.

Many women, equally refusing the role of being an ornamental fuchsia because they know they are gorse and mountain ash, *do* set forth into that bright morning. How do they do it? Historically, many of them would take a gun. Robyn Davidson took camels. Donkeys for Dervla Murphy. Isabelle Eberhardt dressed as a man. Maybe other women are not scared in the first place. Or they conquer their fear because they are braver than me.

I can be brave, I wail to myself. Just not about *this*.

I admit I am a bit nesh. I don't like being hungry and I really hate being cold. I don't take serious risks without seriously good reasons. But I can get over every aspect of my weediness for the sake of my dream.

So let me revisit my dream. I want to tell you that I have done it sometimes. I have walked out alone into the hills, strolling till dusk, then grandly tossed my rucksack onto a perfect spot with views right into next week, lit a fire and declared the place mine for the night. That is the truth. But it is not the whole truth. I have got that far, but then I have looked around me and whimpered. Those open hills, those vistas of sheer beauty, the very things that delight me make me exposed. And so I have kicked out the fire, picked up my stuff, and squirrelled myself away in deep woods instead: foetid, too boggy for a fire, the groundsheet arguing with thistles all night and no view of sunrise.

The fear will do that. Almost every woman has been taught a thousand little lessons in being leered at, a hundred unwelcome comments that contaminate us, a dozen nauseating touches, a handful of heart-in-throat times of terror. What do we learn? Fear. Amorphous, pervasive, in-the-marrow fear. When our brothers are learning how to use a map and compass to orient themselves in the wide world, what do we learn? We learn we must live in the narrow world, not the wide one.

It puts my summer dream out of my reach. I am envious of the men who can seize the dream with both hands, watermelon in August, who sleep in ditches and hayricks and barns and get drunk with strangers and hitch rides without panic-stricken hyper-vigilance, who strike up conversations in inns at midnight without fear of anything more than being pickpocketed or bored. They may be anxious about running out of money or sunlight or strength, but not this, the terror we feel.

There is another thing, though, that blocks our common dream, that forbids us all, men as much as women, from sucking the summer for all its juices. As I write, proposed laws would make wild camping a criminal offence. To be asleep under the stars is our birthright. Beyond our human rights: our very animal rights demand that we can do that. It appals me to lose it. A dormouse can. And a hare. Every bird does it and is allowed to do it. To sleep where it chooses, in hedgerows and woods. Just when, as Nick Hayes argues so spiritedly and profoundly in *The Book of Trespass*, we should seize more and more rights of access and roaming, we are losing the few we have.

Even our legal right to walk the footpaths is being lost by fact if not by law. All walkers know how footpaths are frequently blocked. A broken fridge-freezer, three slaughtered badgers, rolls of barbed wire, thorn hedges left unpruned, thickets of brambles and a pile of rusting broken car parts, a wall with jagged edges of broken glass.

Last summer, I took a ten-year-old out for a bike ride. I showed him how to find our place on the map, and told him how we were allowed to bike on bridleways. His eyes shone. He picked it up in minutes, telling me with glee that if we had enough food we could cycle for weeks. He picked out a bridleway on the map. He led us, correctly, to the exact place it was on the land. Heroic pride.

'Right here,' he said.

I checked the map. He was absolutely right. And it was closed off by thick thorn hedges, walls of brambles. It was a steep disappointment for him on his first try.

'Never mind,' I said. 'It happens sometimes. It shouldn't, but it does. Some landowners are . . .' I decided not to finish my thought out loud.

He found another bridleway. The same thing happened. Now he looked really upset. More than disappointed, he had been betrayed. The great promise of summer-freedom had been offered to him and then snatched away. The best consolation I could offer was to suggest that under the circumstances it was fair enough to sit down on the grass verge just where the bridleway had been blocked, and to shout as loudly as possible the end of my sentence about landowners: '. . . fucking BASTARDS'. I sort of hoped the landowner could hear.

Licence to swear as loudly as we liked made the boy grin, but it was a sorry and insufficient recompense.

'Shall we try again?' I asked, but he looked down, muted, as if the failure had been his, and said quietly, 'No.' I really wish the landowner could have heard that.

He was denied his right of passage. For teenagers, finding the Path they can follow, away from home, is also a rite of passage. Perhaps it is the coinciding of summer with adolescence, perhaps it is fledgling freedom from the parental nest: however it happens, the urge to migrate hits teenagers hard. From a student's 'gap-year' to the Indigenous Australian tradition of the 'Walkabout', it is a necessary part of growing up, where the passage of life is echoed by a passage of travel. The fairy tales know it as the Quest, to leave in search of adventure, setting out to seek your fortune, Dick Whittington, tucking his belongings into a red-spotted handkerchief. It is about seeking and searching, finding the world and selfness as *Le Grand Meaulnes* evokes, the sublime and subtle tale of teenage summer nights with the masque, the unknownness and the memory where the boy setting out is 'mysterious, a stranger, in the middle of an unknown world.'

Teenagers, strangers to themselves as much as others, are islands in the middle of their unknown worlds: islands unto themselves, and often seeming as islands to others. D.W. Winnicott writes: 'The boy and girl at puberty can be described ... as an isolate.' My hand-drawn island created by my teenage dreams was an explicit example. This was my island-self. 'People' happen off the island. Self-isolating as a way to find your own path, to become, in an islanded cocoon, who you really seek to be. The teenage isolate walks out, escapes and runs away. She or he is an isolate both from their family and from the places they visit. Stranger, exile, visitor, alien, migrant, traveller, misfit, explorer.

If summer nights and early summer mornings are for the teenagers, the later hours are for the middle-aged. 'Summer afternoon — summer afternoon; to me those have always been the two most beautiful words in the English language,' wrote Henry James, in his early middle-age. This is no longer the drunken languor of the young stealing roses and kisses, but the comfortable ease of the middle-aged. The National Trust tea room. Falling asleep in deckchairs by the roses that you own. It is postprandial, full of lunch and cake. Satisfied (albeit needing a pee). It is the not-really-going-anywhere time. It shares the outlook of Winnie-the-Pooh and sorts well with small children as well as the middle-aged. The adolescents find it *un-fucking-bearable*.

I write all this as if summer were true. It used to be true. Bits of it are still true. Teenagers still feel that tug, compelled to set out and discover a world. The summer sun will always hold its utmost authority at solstice. I will always be honeysuckled in June. At least I think so. But nothing now is certain. The seasons are disordered and the almanac confounded.

Plants sense both air and soil temperature. Many need winter cold before they can burst out into summer: a process called vernalisation. When winters are not cold enough, the germination of some plants will be affected. Pests and diseases of native trees are more likely to survive warmer winters. If spring arrives too early, trees may move into leaf earlier and leaf-eating caterpillars will come earlier. But the birds that depend on those caterpillars, the blue tit, great tit and pied flycatcher, don't lay their eggs earlier, and may go hungry. Their chicks' predators, in turn – the sparrowhawks and the stoats, for example – will have less food.

And the idea of summer *is* sinister now. Too much the heat. Too much the melting. No longer the melting into each other's arms, but the cruel melting of ice nearly three miles deep. The meltwater that floods into the seas that can only rise and rise. Implacable. Inevitable. The little Hebridean island by Skye will be part-flooded. Its island-child will be drowned. The islands that magnetised millions every summer – the Maldives, Martinique, the Seychelles – are first anxious then angered then terrified then gone.

The age-old promise to the young is that they may set out on a midsummer morning, and that if they learn those folktale virtues – be kind, be curious, be canny, be coura- geous – they will find their fortune. Implicit in this is the promise that while they are changing, growing, reaching their full height, rising to the occasion every midsummer morning, they are doing so in a stable world, where the ground will not give way under their feet, where the path will not crumble at the cliff edge, where land and sky and water each hold their bounds, where time and season rhyme.

Rites of passage are – and should be – about an individual loss of innocence in order to learn the fuller knowledge of the next stage of life, but the young today are having to learn that the very world around them is in passage, a seasick kind of instability. For them, the correct maps are not the OS maps detailing ancient pathways, but rather future maps, showing coastal erosion as the seas rise and where all the horizons are bleak and every melting is an anxiety. For them is granted neither freedom nor glee but the necessity to see into the fear of things. The fear that surpasses any personal fear. Summer itself is overshadowed now.

Somewhere, it is Still Summer

Tishani Doshi

Summer is the long stretch. The arm of return. After the perseverance of winter and the breakthrough of spring, we are finally here again. The days are as long as they will ever be. For some, there is no remembrance of summer rain. For others, the rain is inconsequential. Still, it is a season of water – of trips to the seaside, of donning wellies to muck about in the brooks that run alongside the village, of building a dam across the river and thrashing around in it till you are pink from the sun.

We are in Nercwys, a village in Flintshire, North Wales. The summers in question range from 1951 to 2014, but we net over them all, until they are layered one over the other, a palimpsest of time, of summers.

In the 1950s, Nercwys was a village of 300. Thirty years later, when I began going there, the population hadn't greatly changed. It is like one of those Fisher-Price villages my siblings and I built at home in Madras, in India, which is nothing like a Fisher-Price village. In Nercwys, the houses on the main road stand like matchboxes in a straight line. There are farms in the surrounding hills, a post office and a shop where you can buy Smarties, and everyone knows everyone else. The entire village of Nercwys could fit into an apartment building in Madras.

My mother was born in January 1947, one of the coldest winters on record. There is a story of her father bringing her home from the hospital on his bicycle. I imagine it – a scene from a moody black-and-white film, bare trees lining the streets banked with snow. She was named Eira Gwyneth, which translates from the Welsh as Snow White. In 1968, when she arrived in India to marry my father, after both families reconciled to their relationship, her name was considered a good omen because my father's father's cement-based paint company was also called Snow White.

My mother is reticent to share her memories. It's as though she thinks they will turn into something else or disappear if she says them out loud. In a biography of R.S. Thomas, I read about an interview he gave to the *Independent on Sunday* saying, 'I don't want fingers poked into my life. I don't know what they can unearth.'

My mother doesn't say it, but I understand she doesn't want my fingers poking about in her life.

She tells me to speak to her childhood friend, Rhona Cowell, instead, saying Rhona would remember it well. I speak to Rhona and to my Uncle Glyn, my mother's oldest brother, whose memory is so capacious he can even recall the tagline of his favourite treat shop in Rhyl: *CLWYD ICES: OFTEN LICKED, NEVER BEATEN.*

My first memory of summer in Wales is snow. Although, this is probably late April, the cusp of summer. I can't remember now whether it's my sister or me who draws back the curtains, whether it is she who points, *look look*, and understands exactly what we are seeing and knows what to name it. I know that most mornings since, I have drawn the curtains of whichever room I happen to be sleeping in to see what kind of adventure the day will bring.

We build a snowman with our grandmother, whom we call Nain. He is quite watery. It is late-season flitty snow, which melts as it falls, but there is much excitement about putting on a hat and mittens, of picking up the cold earth and fashioning a person out of it.

Many years later, walking with my mother in a different season in the Theosophical Society in Madras, I ask about my father's ancestral village in Anjar, Gujarat, where his grandparents lived, the place of my father's summers as a boy. Their house was destroyed in the Bhuj earthquake of 2001, long after they'd both died, but I remember walking down the street from that house and getting my ears pierced in a jeweller's shop. A man with hairy ears and a Nehru cap used a needle to put gold in my ears and gave me a gift of small glinting scissors afterwards. I claim this as my earliest memory but my mother says it didn't happen that way. She says my sister and I had our ears pierced at a jeweller's in Madras, and they used a gun, not a needle. There was no gift of silver scissors in exchange for the pain. She tells me that the last time we went as a family to Gujarat was in 1981, before we travelled to Wales; that we must have stayed in a hotel as the house in Anjar wouldn't have had room for us all. She tells me it's where I picked up lice and gave them to my cousins Dan and Jon, and it was only after Nain said, 'Why does this girl keep scratching her head?' that the lice were found out.

1981: summer of snow and lice. Also, the summer Prince Charles got married to Lady Di, whose wedding I remember watching on TV, although this could also be a fake memory. I buy a Lady Di picture book and I dream of Lady Di hats, and when I get back home to Madras I put a mosquito net over my head as though it were a wedding veil and I prance through the house pretending to be her.

The main road of Nercwys is a parade of identical terraced houses – smart, upright, with small front gardens and a shed and backyard. My Nain and Taid live at Number 10, Tan-y-Rhos. Taid died in 1977, but we still refer to it as Nain and Taid's.

Down the road from Tan-y-Rhos there is a playground with swings and a rocking horse and a roundabout. The playground is surrounded by fields where spotted cows stand in clusters. My sister and I walk to the playground and back by ourselves. We meet the other children from the village, for whom this is their always life. For my sister and I, this is our place of sometimes summers.

In India I know the arrival of night as something harsh and sudden, darkness flooding the room with the Bootchie-Man and all the other attendants of fear. In Wales, we play on and on, past mealtimes, past bedtime. I remember our parents coming to fetch us once from the playground saying how late it was and had we forgotten about the time?

In my mind that evening expands into multiple evenings of summer abandon. A feeling that time has ceased to exist, or that you are surpassing it somehow by the fact of being alive. Summer is that feeling for me. The playground in Nercwys is like Dali's painting *The Persistence of Memory*, shape-shifting, slipping between cracks of dream and reality, a place where I can meet my mother as a young girl playing on the swings, a crater of timelessness.

My Uncle Glyn is telling me how his big thrill as a boy was to find a box of matches because you could *do* stuff with them. His friends and he once set a hedge on fire. 'Our reaction was quite simple,' he says, 'we just ran like hell.' This is Glyn's grandson Mylo's favourite story of *the olden days*.

I speak to Glyn and Rhona in November 2020 when the UK is in the midst of a month-long lockdown. The word they both use to define their summer childhoods in semi-rural Wales is 'freedom', the opposite of what they've been going through this year with the coronavirus and its constraints.

To hear their stories, you'd think they lived in a Welsh version of an Enid Blyton book. Picnics by the River Terrig with lemonade and sandwiches, rambling in bluebell woods, daring each other to jump off hay bales and pigeon lofts. Playing cricket and rounders and Foxes and Hounds. Making bows and arrows and peashooters, building tree cabins and playing in the cinder banks by the old vicarage. Constable Jones from neighbouring Gwernymynydd cycling through, making his presence known, especially during harvest time when red apples started to ruby the trees, and naughty children were tempted to go scrumping. Was there ever a more delightful word than scrumping?

Rhona says they were always going on adventures, collecting tadpoles up in the fields near Rhos Ithel, gathering primroses and blackberries, putting on pantomimes for their parents. There was a piece of land, Pen-y-Bryn, which used to be an old quarry and had a sign to keep trespassers out, where they spent many happy hours hidden away from the world. They were never desperate to fill time, Glyn says. One day followed the rest and there were always daft things to do like setting a hedge on fire. He says he can still feel the tiredness at the end of those days. The sunburnt pink legs. His mother asking, 'What have you been doing?'

In the early 2000s when I'm living in London, I tell some-one I'm half-Welsh, that I spent summers going to Rhyl to ride the beach donkeys and whoosh down the slides at the Sun Centre, and the person says, 'Oh, poor you,' which perplexes me.

My mother spent the first years of her life in a house called Tyn-y-Groes, or the Crossing House, in Nercwys. Six people lived in that house. It had one bedroom and no electricity. There were two taps – one in the back and one in the washhouse. There was a decent-sized garden where my Taid grew vegetables, and once a week a metal tub would be dragged in for baths. In the mid-fifties the family moved to Tan-y-Rhos, one of the council houses on the main road, which was compact but had two floors, three bedrooms and eventually, an indoor bathroom.

All through my childhood, I had believed in the rich-ness of my mother's childhood. I grew up in the pre-liber-alised India of the 1980s, in Madras, that most conservative and low-key of India's big cities, which even though it housed millions, had all the languor of an R.K. Narayan novel. Wales was my elsewhere. I conflated Wales with England, as a place where things happened, where you could buy the most beautiful things. My mother's relatives would send packages for Christmas, and if they didn't go missing in the post, they held treasures: knickers from Marks & Spencer's, scented soaps in the shape of shells, Mars bars, toilet bags with pink stripes, neon stuff with giant bows. I still sometimes walk into Hamleys on Regent Street to see whether I'll be hit by that same flash of childhood greed and excitement (in fact, I'm steamroll-ered by fatigue). During our short London interludes, before getting the train from Euston to Chester, I remember the dizziness of being in Hamleys, our parents telling us we could get one toy each, the agony of the decision because wherever you looked there was something utterly shiny and wantable. Would it be the Sindy dressing table or a Skipper doll? I think of hauling that one toy to my Nain and Taid's carpeted house in Nercwys where the television had so many channels (four!), and the pantry was stocked with Ribena and chocolate digestives, and the bathroom at the top of the stairs had a bathtub in which we could make bubbles, and how all this seemed like a luxurious fairy tale to me.

It is only after reading Jan Morris's *Wales: Epic Views of a Small Country*, that I begin to contextualise my childhood memories within a larger socio-economic and colonial history. Morris writes about the endless labour of Welsh miners, quarrymen, tunnellers, sheep farmers. 'All over Wales,' she writes, 'you will find such places, scrawny places, little desolations, signs of the immemorial process by which mankind has extracted the wealth from the substance of this country, cleaned a corner out and moved on ... copper, or manganese, or tin, or iron, or gold, or coal: the industries of Wales have nearly all been brutally extractive. One by one they have burst into activity, made a few people rich, mostly foreigners ... then having exhausted the matter beneath, declined into lifelessness: and so in every part of the country, like the scabs of old wounds, those countless workings remain today dead and abandoned, cherished only by industrial archaeologists ...'

My Taid worked as a shot-firer in a limestone quarry. Glyn explains the system to me. What you'd see when you looked at the quarry was a cliff of white stone that's been cut into. The way you got the white stone down was by drilling perpendicular holes along the hillside and putting explosives down those holes. The stone would then be sent into crushers and packed into lorries to a factory to be mixed with gypsum to make cement. My grandfather didn't do the drilling of the holes, but he set up the explosives. Before the shot was fired, a siren went off, and then the whole face of the cliff would collapse. Glyn remembers how Taid was off work for a month once because a stone had dislodged and broken his leg. My grandfather spent thirty years working in the same quarry. For Glyn's generation, the aspiration was to get a job where you could put on a tie and work indoors. Your parents would be proud of you if you could be a teacher, for instance, or an insurance agent.

I keep thinking about the scabs of old wounds that Jan Morris writes about. How she says they'd be cherished only by industrial archaeologists, and yet so many of Glyn and Rhona's childhood summer memories are set in this post-extraction Welsh landscape. The abandoned quarries or mines were an escape, a setting for other worlds. They both talked about building a dam over the River Terrig using debris from a nearby mine. Glyn says no one could really swim, but they dived in anyway. Sometimes they'd find small coal mines in the surrounding areas, which were open cast, which means that coal had been extracted from the side of the mountain, leaving only the streaky lines of coal behind. Those holes were an excellent place to play hide and seek or cowboys and Indians. He describes the cinder blocks – coal that had been taken out and fired, eight or twelve feet high, huge apocalyptic blocks atop which they sat and watched the world. Sometimes a grass snake would slither by, sometimes an adder.

Rhona tells me of how a favourite place to gather in summer was the smithy to watch Ted and Josh shoe the horses. She remembers the smell of the burning, their voices keeping the horses calm. How summer was the time of harvesting, the men stacking up the trailers and tractors with bales of hay and the children riding on top ('no such thing as health and safety then'), how there was a long drainage pipe which they dared themselves to crawl through ('gives me horrors now'). Sometimes, she says, they'd find themselves walking in the same direction as a herd of Jersey cows, and the farmer would throw her on the back of one for a ride.

Mostly, they looked for things to do that were free. Bikes had to be borrowed if you wanted adventures further afield and they were usually adult bikes so you had to be able to stand and pedal. Sometimes your mother would give you a shilling and you could get the bus to Mold for the cinema and a treat. And a couple of times a week there was the delight of queueing up at the visiting ice-cream van for a lolly.

I think of my Welsh grandfather who exploded cliffs in order to make cement, and my Indian grandfather who manufactured cement-based paint, how these two men who never met one another are cemented together in some way. They had the same ethic for hard work, for saving, for prayer, and I remember them being serious, or perhaps it's because all the photographs of that time freeze people in a moment of concern.

I think of my parents and their siblings, growing up in the hard years after WWII, experiencing a kind of prosperity later in their lives so far removed from their childhoods and their parents' entire lives. How if you've grown up that way you have definite ideas about what constitutes work, which is why my mother's other brother, Uncle Haydn, always rolled his eyes when any of us nieces or nephews said we were going into things like French or poetry or freelancing. 'When are you going to get a real job?' he'd say. I think about how we are made up of the generations before us and how nothing is thrown away. How when we meet it is always in the season of summer.

Inger Christensen, writing about her summers near Munkebjerg in Denmark between 1939–1949, describes them as 'a morass of luxuriance'. For her the most powerful summer experience was a feeling of warmth filling your body so completely till there was no boundary between the air and your skin. She writes how summer becomes apparent through a string of images and experiences that begin to stand out so as to make them seem almost supernatural. For her, it's these three images: 'open, endless beauty; pointless energy; and the security of not being alone.'

I grew up in a place of endless summer. The only season to mark a change in Madras was the monsoon, which periodically arrived with cyclones. So, the opposite of summer was not winter, but warm, sometimes life-threatening rain. Still, I identify with Christensen's distinctly northern hemisphere notion of summer, its great blanket of warmth, perhaps because of my summers in Wales, but also because the memory of summer begins in childhood, and in some ways remains there.

Summer is a break from uniforms and timetables when the world hangs just outside your window and you flit from ennui to joy. Time is untrammelled. The days go on and on, sometimes interminably, sometimes dazzlingly, and in all this time there is always some element of shedding and transformation at play. I remember returning from summer back to my life in Madras, desperate to reveal my new self to my old friends, wondering how their summers had altered them. Summer can be generous, an unending field interrupted by apertures, so it is possible to hitch your load of memories to someone else's.

I can see my Uncle Glyn going over to Barry Evans's house and asking his mother if he's around to play. Barry and Glyn clearing nettles in Plas Onn Hall all morning for a few shillings. Here they are playing cricket in the fields and sometimes on the road, which they're not meant to do as it's dangerous. Tearing through the woods, always racing, except when it's time to go home to eat, and there, perhaps, something calmer, a solitary moment with the John Bull magazines, chortling at the stories of someone called P.G. Wodehouse.

I can see a band of young Welsh girls, my mother and her sister Menna among them, leaving at first light to go mushrooming, the village quiet except for the bleating and mooing of new lambs and calves, returning for breakfast with baskets full of porcinis and chanterelles. Now they are rambling over the moors and the horseshoe pass on the Women's Institute mystery tour, drinking lemonade and tea, squatting down in the heather for a wee, the crackle and hiss.

Here is Nain up at five to make sandwiches for the family's annual outing to the seaside. It's a warm August day and they will be one of the first at the station. There will be the usual excitement, the children rushing to the bridge to watch the train come in, leaning over to put their faces in the vapour of steam. Taid wears a tweed sports jacket and flannels. You don't flaunt yourself on the beaches. When they get there, they'll stop at Beach Teas for something restorative. There'll be time for donkeys later, but for most of the day the grown-ups sit and keep watch. They don't go anywhere near the water. The children tear up and down in circles, build sandcastles and paddle in the waves, and turn up when they need a sandwich. What would the British be without sandwiches?

Here is my Nain again. It's 6 June 1967. She's standing on the Liverpool Docks waving goodbye. Her daughter Eira, who is only twenty years old, is going off to Canada with her friend Margaret. The two girls are wearing matching blue coats that they've bought on the ship because they're already cold. Her son Glyn and her daughter Menna stand beside her. Now the *Empress of Canada* is off. There's bunting and people are waving and Nain is in tears. She doesn't know when she'll see her daughter again. When they reach Montreal, the girls realise there isn't a great demand for English shorthand typists so they hop on a train to Toronto and from there they send letters home with local newspapers and photographs of what they're doing, and Nain says, 'Who's this? Looks like an Indian lad in these photos . . .'

Now the whole village is filing in. It is 2 June 1953, Queen Elizabeth's coronation. My mother's friend Julie's house has one of the few televisions in the village. I see all my aunties and uncles – Ken, Norman, Beryl, Heddwyn, Betty, Eirlys, all of them are younger versions of themselves, wearing clothes that are sturdy and handstitched. The children are on the floor and the adults gather around. A collective witnessing.

Here is my entire family outside The Butchers Arms in Nercwys. It is June 2014. I have been married six months and I've brought my Italian husband to my mother's village, to visit my Nain and Taid's grave in the cemetery of St Mary's, to show him the playground. There must be fifty of us or more. We are standing on the grass, drinking beer and gin and tonics. Children are running about and we move from one person to the next, trying to fill the years with a few sentences about our lives. There's a photograph in which we are all aglow and squinting. The next day we wake to find soft pink stripes across our foreheads. You never think you're going to get sunburned in Wales.

Imagine a village where everyone knows everyone else. Where all the people are white and you either go to Welsh chapel or English church, and the only people of colour you've seen are the Indian gentlemen who come through in the summertime with their cases of silks. You think they must come from the other side of the world, but they are probably from Birmingham or Manchester, which may as well be the other side of the world. The Indian gents come through during summer with the other foreigners – the Irish tinkers who sell heather for good luck and tell you your fortune, and the Frenchman on his bicycle they call Johnny Onions. It is a working-class village with only the vicar being 'slightly above'. Imagine then going off to grammar school in Chester, and a boy called Peter Dunn invites you to his house to listen to records, and it must have been Elvis that everyone was listening to that year, but the thing you remember is not the music but the house and the car. Never in your life have you met anyone who lives in a house this huge and has a car.

Jan Morris writes of the Welsh that they aren't as a people 'natural cosmopolitans'. Compared to most European countries, the number of Welsh emigrants is small. In the nineteenth century, the proportion of emigrants is four times bigger in England, seven times bigger in Scotland and twenty-six times bigger among the Irish. Morris describes the Welsh as a 'people of intense collective instinct, agonizingly prone to homesickness ... many a Welsh emigrant has come home again to die or publish his memoirs. Among those who stick it out abroad life is shot through often by an insatiable pining for the sounds, colours, feelings and suggestions of the Welsh landscape.'

My mother and father met in Toronto, and after a romance they both went back to their respective homes and wrote letters to each other every day for six months until on Guy Fawkes Day, 1968, my mother flew to India and changed her life. For three years she sent letters and photographs home. In the summer of 1971, she brought her Indian husband Vinod to Wales. My father was the first brown person the people of Nercwys had had tea with.

Before their children had grown up, my Nain and Taid had never left Britain, but all their four children travelled far, unimaginably far – New Zealand, the British Virgin Islands, America, India. All of them looped back to live in Britain except for my mother who stayed in India. Nain came to India only once, in 1978. It was her first time on a plane. They took her from Kashmir to Kanyakumari – there are pictures of them on ponies and in houseboats, one cherished photograph of all us squashed onto a sofa in Madras. Nain said she only wanted to see how and where her daughter lived; after that, she was content to stay in Wales.

I did not learn the word *hiraeth* from my mother. Certain words enter the English vocabulary because they represent something untranslatably beautiful, but begin to lose potency each time the word is uttered, like *kintsugi* (the Japanese art of repairing broken pottery), or *hygge* (a Danish kind of cosiness). In the same way, the word *hiraeth* – that deep Welsh longing – has been overused. Still, I remember the first time I heard it and felt a small detonation. The idea that you could long for an idea of home, which may not even exist, resonated with a favourite line from Carson McCullers: 'We are homesick most for the places we have never known.'

Everything I've known of Wales has been given to me in shards, photographs, unreliable slivers of time. When my sister and I went off to university in America, our some-times summers in Nercwys ended. I'd wing my way back to the UK regularly, but my base was London. I'd go to Hay-on-Wye for the Hay Festival, and I visited Aberystwyth and Carmarthenshire. I even spent a few nights in Dylan Thomas's childhood house on 5 Cwmdonkin Drive in Swansea, exploring Laugharne and the coast – Caswell Bay, where he probably canoodled with his girlfriend Pamela and all the country pubs he got thrown out of for misbe-having, taking deep inhalations of that air he described as 'the odour of rabbits' fur after rain.' I read the *Mabinogion* and was beginning to understand the Celtic connection between land and myth, but I was looking at it from the outside. The real connection was not something I inher-ently felt via the land or poetry, but it was through memory and family, and so everything lay contained in that small village of Nercwys.

The house I've been living in for the past ten years on a beach in Tamil Nadu is called Ar Lan y Môr (Beside the Sea), and when I'm back there after some time away, I blast Bryn Terfel's recording as I cut through the scrubby drive, watching a bright kingfisher swoop by or an emerald-green bee-eater sunning itself on the brick wall. The neem trees spread horizontally like a rash of green because the salt wind stunts their growth and the rattle of a black-rumped flameback layers the soundtrack with its own noise, and somehow this becomes my *hiraeth* because it's what I long for most when I'm away. This feeling of entering a scene that is as close to that childhood summer in Wales, a feeling of timelessness.

Jan Morris introduces me to the other spectrum of *hiraeth*, which is *hwyl*. The Welsh fluctuate, she says, between extremes – exuberance and desolation. 'Sometimes when you look out of a Welsh window all seems lost – or if not lost at least permanently suspended in a hangdog limbo. The drizzle seems never likely to stop, the mountains look permanently concealed in mist, the sea is grey and queasy, the town damp and dingy – you can bet your life it's early closing day. The sheep in the field out there are huddled miserably against the wind. The river roars sullenly beyond the wood. Nothing, one feels, is ever going to change, or even perhaps to happen. But then suddenly out of the west a fine bright breeze comes marching in, and everything is different ... Is there anywhere on earth to beat Wales? you ask yourself then.'

I imagine what it must be like to grow up on the edge of a place like this in the fifties and sixties, how it might occasionally feel as though you were in a kind of exile. I can remember feeling like this growing up in the '70s and '80s in Madras, longing to be part of a larger world.

There is a photograph of Nain and Taid in a frame in Madras. Taid looks like my mother wearing a suit. They have the same oval face and high forehead. I have the same oval face and high forehead.

I don't know when I'll return to Nercwys. My Uncle Haydn still lives in the village with his partner Jean, and there are other aunties, uncles, cousins, although, as each year goes by, the roster diminishes. I remember the feeling of being inside my Nain and Taid's house so clearly. It is childhood, it is summer. There's a barometer on the wall which tells you what kind of a day it's going to be. The milkman has left glass bottles of milk on the doorstep. I sleep in a bunk bed and have to go on the bottom because at night I sleep too hard and sometimes roll off the bed. And that is summer too. The ever-present chance of danger. The way you're struck by a sudden cold stream of water when you're out in the ocean and feel you're being pulled away. It's the stories of boys who hit their heads while diving in the river and men who go off for walks with their rifles and 'accidentally' shoot themselves. You never know how close you are to this danger, but later, in your grown-up life, you look back and wonder how you made it this far. Summer is also about secrets. Some of which you'll never know, because summer is when you grow up in your body, which is as free as it will ever be, but you must learn to keep things between you. There are some hints — the handsome caretaker's son of Plas Onn who plays music on the Dansette record player, the Scout group from Merseyside who pitch up in summer with their smart uniforms, the giant steamrollers tarmacking the road, filling your nostrils with the strong smell of tar. It's the experiences you're having and the experiences you long to have. Not just the Shrewsbury Flower Show or the Llangollen Eisteddfod but one day you are going to be performing in the Royal Albert Hall in London!

Summer is unrelenting. The day is too busy, demanding to be lived. Later you will have a litany of questions, but there may not be anyone to answer them. Like how did Nain and Taid meet? Because what we know is so little. That Nain worked on the other side of Wrexham in a munitions factory during the war making parachutes and Taid was a shot-firer and the deacon in the chapel, and they got married in 1942, but we can't know how or where because it's not what you asked. It's how the family worked. There weren't a lot of discussions. Things were just done, then you moved on. There was no great build-up. It was enough that your parents felt you had enough about you to take care of yourself. Once, maybe twice, you found them standing at the gate in the darkening. You don't have a watch so it's easy to forget, and they say, where've you been?

It's late. And you go inside all together, and the house takes you in. Summer is what you look forward to. When it ebbs away and the nights grow darker you know there are things you can do to get through the winter, but what you're really preparing for is your next go at summer.

AUTUMN

Your Shrouded Form

Luke Turner

October's bellowing anger breaks and cleaves
The bronzed battalions of the stricken wood
In whose lament I hear a voice that grieves
For battle's fruitless harvest, and the feud
Of outraged men. Their lives are like the leaves
Scattered in flocks of ruin, tossed and blown
Along the westering furnace flaring red.
O martyred youth and manhood overthrown,
The burden of your wrongs is on my head.

'Autumn', written in Craiglockhart, 1917
– Siegfried Sassoon

It can take a century after a tree's death for its skeleton to rot away. In Sanctuary Wood, a short drive from the Belgian town of Ypres, young silver birch and middle-aged beech tower over a tree stump jagged as a fairy-tale mountain range. The decaying trunk is girdled by loops of barbed wire, stuck with poppies and crosses, and sits in a small copse that was the scene of heavy fighting around the Ypres Salient during the 1914 to 1918 war. I encountered the stump, nature's cenotaph to the war dead, on an October afternoon in the mid-1990s, during a school battlefields trip. Teenage historians freed from the classroom, we scampered around the trenches and rusting bits of corrugated iron that are supposedly the remains of the British and Canadian front line, now preserved by the Hill 62 museum. It felt exciting, this site of violence, compared to the sombre melancholy of the regiments of white headstones in the huge cemeteries that punctuate the flat Flanders landscape like ivory dominoes abandoned on green baize. I remember the dreich and the drizzle and the falling leaves, our teacher telling us about reliable evidence and primary sources. Someone else said that 'Fat Jacques', the museum's founder, used to water the trenches for authentic mud, and the 'shell holes' scattered through the woodland occasionally had sharper edges, as if freshly touched up with a spade.

The trip to the battlefields of France and Belgium was a rare event to look forward to at the start of the depressing autumn term of the fifth year. The carefree weeks of the summer holiday had ended with a return to the tedious grimness of an all-boys state school, the whiff of Lynx deodorant and petty macho aggravation, bullies sizing up those of us arriving for the new term in a second-hand uniform blazer several sizes too large. It was also the dreaded season when the former grammar with delusions of middle-class establishment grandeur forced us to play rugby. So Mr Jones's history class went from the playing fields of a mid-sized comprehensive by coach to France and Belgium to do what teenage boys, freed from parental constraints, tend to do — misbehave, indulge petty prejudice, think about girls. Shopkeepers long immune to repeated visits from English lads with artificially lowered voices and fuzzy chins refused to sell stubby bottles of lager. Some tried to work out if they could force the coach loo to perform an emergency discharge as we crossed the border into France, a dirty protest upgrade on xenophobic back window mooning. The driver was a creep, switching on the tannoy to announce through a voice cracked by regular access to duty-free cigarettes, 'Eyes left — lovely bit of crumpet out there boys,' every time we drove past girls our age walking to school, much to the consternation of the teachers. In the evening someone produced a handheld Sony games console. It had a TV adapter, and we climbed a rickety metal tower, part of some long-condemned adventure playground, to see if we could get a signal, convinced that late-night European telly would be wall-to-wall pornography. As we stood on the swaying scaffold staring wistfully at the small screen of static, I endured the added frisson of a deep and unrequited crush on one of my classmates, his tanned summer face lit by the soft glow. Later, in the youth hostel dormitories that we were told to imagine were barracks for the British Expeditionary Force in 1915, I longed for his body, a bunk away in the darkness.

Looking back, I wish our battlefields trip had been experienced with the knowledge that millions of boys our age

– sixteen, seventeen at a push – fought and died on the Western Front. Contemporary research suggests that in Britain alone as many as 250,000 boys under the age of nineteen were caught up in the wave of patriotic optimism that swept the country in the autumn of 1914. Some would have rushed to the recruiting station in a gang of their mates, peer pressure always a prime motivator for teenage boys. They lied about their ages for love of king and country, for adventure, to escape the misery of poverty at home. The war, after all, would be 'over by Christmas'. It probably felt as if it'd all be a right laugh. Now, it's sickening to look at an old black-and-white photograph of a soldier like Aby Bevistein, his handsome and youthful face peering intently from underneath a peaked cap that looks several sizes too big. Bevistein, a Polish émigré who came to England and changed his name to Harris before enlisting in the British army, died aged seventeen, killed not by the Germans, but shot for 'cowardice' by his own side. His wasn't a story we were told as the coach drove us around to peer at craters, cemeteries, museums, and areas of woodland still surrounded by fences with signs in three languages that warned of unexploded munitions.

The First World War was taught in battles and numbers, not feelings and certainly not the complexities of lust. As my teenage years went on, my fluid sexuality took over from what I thought was a childlike interest in war. Men who liked men weren't supposed to spend hours poring over maps of old battlefields, or so I thought. I rejected this fascination as I explored the hinterlands of queer sex

– obsessing over war and history felt incongruous with this compulsive drive to live in the heated present of desire. To still be building model kits and reading war novels felt *too straight*. It was all no doubt tied up with complex and internalised prejudices, slowly absorbed from a homophobic society that believes that men who like men are in some way not fully men, are not fighters, are not brave.

It took me by surprise when all this once more came to the fore. My childhood fascination with war ran alongside, but occasionally intersected with, a love of the outdoors. The maps I blue-tacked to my bedroom wall had, after all, first been developed by the Ordnance Survey to get a better military and tactical understanding of Britain's topography. While researching my memoir *Out of the Woods*, trying to make sense of how my turbulent sexual identity connected to our long human relationship with forests and woodlands, I came across Siegfried Sassoon's wartime poem 'Autumn', with which this essay begins.

Most First World War nature poetry focuses on the contrast between the glories of spring and the horrors of mechanised violence, but 'Autumn' is a very different kind of poem. As I started to explore Sassoon's life and work, I encountered a vivid tenderness in his writing about both nature and men. I read in both his verse and his barely fictionalised account of trench life *Memoirs of an Infantry Officer*, an understanding of the complexity of male existence in appalling circumstances. It had a sensuality as well as an empathy, a sense of longing that struck me as being, for its time, deeply radical and queer.

Western Front war art and literature were shaped by the logic of military action. If war poetry often seems to be set in springtime and summer, that is because this was when the heaviest fighting took place. The warmth, clear weather and drier ground of the spring and summer made them the seasons for major offensives. As Professor Robert DeCourcy Ward wrote in a strategic analysis published in the *Scientific Monthly* of 1918, 'the summer ... is meteorologically the most favorable season of the year for campaigning on the western front.' The attempts by the allied and German armies to outflank one another in the 'race to the coast' that took place in the autumn of 1914 ground to a halt, becoming mired in the trench warfare that would define the conflict, in part due to the deteriorating weather.

Soldiers therefore had a far higher chance of dying on the Western Front through the summer months, with casualty numbers declining as the leaves turned during October and November. The coming of autumn meant the promise of respite from the major offensives of spring and summer, when whistles commanded them to race across a shell-blasted no-man's-land into a withering rain of machine-gun bullets. The changing of the seasons would have had a strong resonance for so many who fought. My great-grandad, Ted Turner, was gassed during the war, and we were told he was never the same after it. Like many thousands of others on all sides, he was an agricultural labourer, growing up in London's Epping Forest. Men like Ted would no doubt have had an aesthetic response to trees as we do today, but something far deeper too – they were part of his working life, his identity, his sense of place and home. They would have grown up with a consciousness attuned to the role woodland management played in the function of everyday life and traditions, from rights over access to the land to the simple need for firewood for cooking and heating. Their lives were based around the rhythms and patterns of the seasons, doing jobs that required an intimate knowledge of weather, topography, flora and fauna. Many, including Sassoon, wrote wistful letters home or poetry dreaming of an escape to an English pastoral idyll. Whether they were conscious of it or not, for many, the British landscape played a role in providing a narrative for why they were fighting in the first place.

In the long centuries of English military adventure and colonisation, woodlands were at the core of the martial sense of nationhood. On a practical level, so many trees were required to build the ships of Imperial expansion and national defence that there was deep disquiet about the nation's ability to sustain its navy. John Evelyn's 1664 polemic *Silva or a Discourse on Forest-Trees* is an early classic of nature writing, directly inspired by his anxieties that an arboreally depleted Britain would be a weakened nation. After the Great Storm of 1703 he wrote, 'I still hear, sure I am that I still feel, the dismal groans of our forests; the late dreadful hurricane having subverted so many thousands of goodly oaks, prostrating the trees, laying them in ghastly postures, like whole regiments fallen in battle by the sword of the conqueror.' His words are an uncanny prefiguring of Sassoon's poem. David Garrick's 1759 song 'Hearts of Oak' performs an act of lyrical joinery connecting the idealised British sailor with the material used to build the ships in which he fought: 'Heart of oak are our ships, heart of oak are our men; / We always are ready, steady, boys, steady! / We'll fight and we'll conquer again and again'. Again, how different from the ruined 'bronzed battalions' of Sassoon's 'Autumn'. 'Hearts of Oak' was a song still popular during the early years of the twentieth century. William Dove was moved by it being played at the end of a cinema show in Shepherd's Bush: 'you know one feels that little shiver run up their back and you know you've got to do something,' he later recalled. The following Monday, he volunteered to join the army. William Dove had only just turned seventeen.

The experience of encountering the familiar changings of the seasons in the carnage of the battlefield would have been traumatic for these men, and spring especially provides an easy shorthand to contrast violence and the fecundity of new life. In Wilfred Owen's poem 'Spring Offensive', men reluctantly pass through an idealised landscape of butter-cups, insect life and trees only to cross a ridge 'to the hot blast and fury of hell's upsurge'. Alan Seeger's 'I Have a Rendezvous with Death' has spring as a time of foreboding and dread, every sylvan image of the season – 'blue days and fair', 'the first meadow-flowers' – a reminder of the return of the fighting season, and the poet's unshakable conviction that death was waiting for him. Seeger was killed during the Battle of the Somme in July 1916.

Birdsong, and especially the skylark in spring, has almost become a cliché of the folk memory of trench life. Larks

appear in John McRae's poem 'In Flanders Field', while
Vaughan Williams' 'The Lark Ascending', written in 1914
and first performed in the years after the armistice, became
forever associated with the memories of halcyon springs of
the pre-war years, the soaring bird as violin delicately
stitching together a dream of an England now in mourn-
ing. At the time, however, some soldiers found the springtime larks to be a painful taunt, a reminder of the violence
of the fighting season. In a letter sent home in 1916, Sergeant
Major Frederic Hillersdon Keeling wrote that, 'Every
morning when I was in the front-line trenches I used to
hear the larks singing soon after we stood-to about dawn.
But those wretched larks made me more sad than almost
anything else out here ... Their songs are so closely associated in my mind with peaceful summer days in gardens in
pleasant landscapes in Blighty. Here one knows the larks
sing at seven and the guns begin at nine or ten ...' Keeling
was killed just months later, at Delville Wood during the
Battle of the Somme.

This deep sensitivity soldiers had to the landscape around
them was first explored in psychological terms by German
artilleryman Kurt Lewin, who went on to be a pioneer of
applied psychology. He wrote *Kriegslandschaft* (*The Landscape
of War*) in 1917 while recovering from battle injuries. In it,
he explains that for soldiers in the zones behind the lines
the familiar sights of villages, woods, farms and so on are 'a
pure peacetime landscape: the area seemed to extend out to
infinity on all sides almost uniformly'. As he moves towards
the front, the soldier feels the world closing in around him:

'Up "ahead" the area seems to have an end, which is followed by a "nothingness"'. In *Memoirs of an Infantry Officer*, Sassoon describes walking towards battle and away from the 'cool showery sound' of a camp shaded by aspens which would wait, indifferent, for another unit to use the shelter of their branches. He writes, 'It must be difficult, for those who did not experience it, to imagine the sensation of returning to a battle area'.

Once closer to the front line and immersed in the labyrinthine system of trenches, horizons were further narrowed by the nature of the fortifications themselves, a recurring theme of war writing and art. R.C. Sherriff's play *Journey's End* is set on an evening during which 'a pale glimmer of moonlight shines down the steps into one narrow corner of the dugout'. Indeed, from *Journey's End* to *Blackadder Goes Forth*, the poignant comedy series from which '90s school children like me acquired most of their knowledge of trench warfare, the narrative largely unfolds in dugouts and bunkers, spaces where the light of the seasons never reaches, where their passing might be remembered only in a chill of the air, mildew, flooding, the stench of male lives clinging on in confined spaces.

The countryside around these fortifications had become entirely subsumed into war. In *Kriegslandschaft*, Lewin explained how aesthetically benign parts of the peacetime terrain now had a new significance: 'Even the relatively large plains that have not been cut up by trenches, which one could very well designate as fields or forests in and of themselves, are not fields and forests in the sense of the normal peacetime landscape ... Rather, all these things have become pure things of combat.'

I've spent hours looking at these landscapes as they are today on Google Maps and StreetView. It seems unreal that so many millions of men died in these huge agricultural prairies, interspersed with tiny villages, isolated farms, and patches of woodland. Aside from the cemeteries, you'd have no idea of the destruction that cut Europe in a gouge of mud from the North Sea to the Swiss border. In a topography of flat plains and gently rolling downland, the hope of the strategists was always that the next offensive would prove to be the decisive breakthrough, penetrating the trench lines to the undefended territory in the rear. This meant that any natural phenomena that offered shelter or a commanding view over the surrounding terrain became strategically vital, to be defended or captured at all costs.

Hills for which tens of thousands of men died are often little more than a barely perceptible rise in the distance. Forested areas were frequently strategically important points for both sides, and some of the war's most significant battles were fought over them. In his 1916 poem 'At Carnoy', Sassoon writes of sacred nature becoming a place of violence and turmoil – 'Tomorrow we must go / To take some cursèd Wood ... O world God made'. In 'Died of Wounds', written a little later, a mortally injured soldier calls out 'Curse the Wood! It's time to go. O Christ, and what's the good? / We'll never take it, and it's always raining'. The names of corpse-strewn copses and forests occur again and again in his war poems and in *Memoirs of an Infantry Officer*.

Some of these woods have gone now, farmers taking advantage of the war's destruction to turn them over to arable land. Those that survive sit on the horizons of Google Street View as I 'drive' through landscapes that, though rural, are entirely modern, less than a century old. Yet to our modern imagination woods are always ancient things, and it's hard to believe that these thick gloomy lines in the pixelated distance were washed away in a matter of hours in the rain of shellfire that heralded any offensive. Sanctuary Wood is a name haunted by a bitter irony.

The destruction of trees during the war, their reduction to the shattered trunks I saw in Sanctuary Wood, is a recurring motif of the paintings of Paul Nash. Before the war, Nash wrote of how he tried to paint trees as if they were people. His wartime letters to his wife Margaret are full of his deep connection to woodland and the conscription of trees into the seasons. Nash's first visit to the Western Front had been in the spring, and in letters home he has a startling appreciation for the uncanny beauty of the war-torn landscape. On 28 February 1917, he wrote to Margaret that 'the days are sunny here & you can feel the spring coming. How good the old woods look'. In his painting 'Spring in the Trenches, Ridge Wood, 1917', Nash paints a landscape beyond a dugout in which the natural world is carrying on with its natural processes regardless of the war – birds flock in the distance, and those trees that remain carry leaves. He enthused that the area he'd been posted to was 'a most desolate ruinous place two months back, today it was a vivid green; the most broken trees even had sprouted somewhere and in the midst, from the depth of the wood's bruised heart poured out the throbbing song of a nightingale.' A while later, he wrote that, 'It sounds absurd, but life has a greater meaning here and a new zest, and beauty is more poignant. I never feel dull or careless, always alive to the significance of nature who, under these conditions, is full of surprises for me.' In this naivety I wonder if we see a reflection of the modern, simplistic engagement with the potentially restorative powers of the natural world. In 1943, Nash asked the Imperial War Museum not to lend 'Spring in the Trenches' to a retrospective exhibition of his work. The season of new life had been a delusion.

Nash was invalided back to Britain after breaking a rib, returning to the front in the autumn of 1917. Now an official war artist, he arrived towards the end of the Battle of Passchendaele, fought over control of key ridges to the south and east of Ypres, including Sanctuary Wood and Hill 62. The offensive started in late July, the allied commanders hoping to take advantage of dry summer weather. Unfortunately, August 1917 was one of the wettest in decades, the problem of heavy rainfall exacerbated by cool, cloudy weather reducing evaporation, and the destruction of drainage systems in the low-lying areas. Autumn had come early, and the battlefield became a quagmire that swallowed, according to some estimates, half a million lives.

What Nash saw in the churned mud of the Passchendaele battlefield would change his perspective, and his paintings, for good. On 13 November 1917, he wrote home of 'the most frightful nightmare of a country more conceived by Dante or

Poe than by nature, unspeakable, utterly indescribable ... no glimmer of God's hand is seen anywhere. Sunrise and sunset are blasphemous, they are mockeries to man ... The rain drives on, the stinking mud becomes more evilly yellow, the shell holes fill up with green-white water, the roads and tracks are covered in inches of slime, the black dying trees ooze and sweat and the shells never cease.'

His words, gothic and violent, would be translated into some of his most memorable paintings. These depict countryside across which war has passed during the spring and summer, leaving a silent autumn of rain and mud, with no balm in the fiery fall of leaves, or fields brushed with golden stubble. Trees are the key subjects of 'Rain: Lake Zillebeke', 'Sunrise Inverness Copse', and 'The Menin Road', in which two soldiers trudge through the oomska, almost indistinguishable from the ruins of a woodland. In them, Lewin's 'pure peacetime landscape' has been ruined by shellfire, trees rise as blasted stumps from water-filled craters that gleam under a sky sinister with heavy clouds or, instead of sun and moon, an exploding flare. His 1918 painting 'Wire' foregrounds a trunk of a tree, its upper branches shattered and gone. It sits in a battlefield of browns and greys, devoid of life, and where there might in peacetime have been a scrub of brambles, nettles and wild roses, rolls of barbed wire tangle the landscape, climbing the broken trunk, a hellish, rusting honeysuckle, a weed of industrialised warfare. It looks eerily similar to the stump of Sanctuary Wood.

Autumn would have been a strange season for the men living in the trenches hidden in Nash's landscapes. The spring and summer fighting season might be over and with it the immense artillery barrages that ended in whistles to call them over the top to meet death chattering from rifles and machine guns, but something more insidious dominated the combat in the winter months. In the mud and the rain, small groups of men were sent across the turgid, sodden waste to cause nuisance, reconnoitre enemy positions, and bring back prisoners for interrogation. Armed with pistols, hand-thrown bombs, knives and bayonets, this is when some of the most vicious hand-to-hand fighting of the war occurred. Sassoon himself was involved with these intimate combats, state-sanctioned street murders carried out in the muddy alleys and dead ends of trenches and dugouts. They appear again and again in his writing.

Sassoon's attitude to war and creative output followed a similar trajectory to that of Nash, from hopeful pastoral idealist to artistic chronicler of imperialist conflict in all its abject grimness. Sassoon joined the army days before the declaration of war in 1914, writing in *Memoirs of a Fox-Hunting Man* that he 'had serious aspirations to heroism in the field'. He spent his youth and young adult life as a member of the gentry, riding and hunting across landscapes shaped by the pastoral ideal that was the foundation of British identity. A riding injury put paid to the twenty-seven-year-old's dream of becoming a cavalry officer. Instead, he served as a Lieutenant in the Royal Welch Fusiliers, seeing at first hand the vain carnage of trench warfare.

The brutal realism of Sassoon's war writing is what makes it striking even to a modern audience. It remains visceral and potent even in the age of multimillion budget films like Sam Mendes's *1917*, or the hyperreal, deep immersion of computer war games. In one of the most horrific sentences I've ever read in war writing, Sassoon describes a scene that would be implausible if it were recreated by special effects: 'Floating on the surface of the flooded trench was the mask of a human face which had detached itself from the skull.' It is an image that I cannot unsee. Sassoon's economical verse and prose illuminate and transcend my memory of the mock-trenches of a cold October woodland, a few miles outside of Ypres.

Sassoon's pen captures the dead, the machines, the insanity, the weather, the structure of the trenches, the surrounding natural world. There's an echo of the muddy and blasted turmoil of Nash's paintings in Sassoon's 'Counter Attack', a blurring between corpses of men and trees – 'the place was rotten with dead; green clumsy legs / High-booted, sprawled and grovelled along the saps / And trunks, face downward, in the sucking mud'. The shared language of arboreal and human physiology is used to describe how both trees and bodies are found dismembered and brutalised by the violence of shellfire, such as in this passage from the *Memoirs*: 'I can remember a pair of hands (nationality unknown) which protruded from the soaked ashen soil like the roots of a tree turned upside down; one hand seemed to be pointing at the sky with an accusing gesture.'

Sassoon never shied away from the gruesome fear and rotting bodies, and the cruelty – 'our chaps were sticking 'em like pigs', he has a soldier saying in 'Remorse'. After all, he was no stranger to the violence himself. After the death of his brother in the failed Gallipoli campaign and dear friends around him, Sassoon earned the reputation as 'Mad Jack' for brave but crazed solo missions of revenge against the Germans. In his diary on 1 April 1916 he wrote, 'Someone told me a year ago that love, sorrow, and hate were things I had never known (things which every poet *should* know!). Now I've known love for Bobbie and Tommy, and grief for Hamo and Tommy, and hate has come also, and the lust to kill ... I used to say I couldn't kill anyone in his war; but, since they shot Tommy, I would gladly stick a bayonet into a German by daylight'. 'Tommy' was David Cuthbert Thomas, a comrade and room-mate with whom Sassoon was infatuated, according to his biographer Jean Moorcroft Wilson, although there is no evidence the love was physically consummated or requited. Nevertheless, the poems written about Thomas glow with affection. In 'A Letter Home', written to his great friend, the writer (and bisexual) Robert Graves, Sassoon describes Thomas as 'one whose yellow head was kissed / By the gods'. Shortly after hearing of his friend's death, Sassoon wrote four lines of verse in his diary: 'For you were glad, and kind, and brave / With hands that clasped me, young and warm / But I have seen a soldier's grave / And I have seen your shrouded form.' The yearning of grief, yes, but in that 'shrouded form' the cruelty too of unrequited love for another man in an age that would not stomach it. I wonder if in the acute appreciation for the fragility of male lives so beautifully depicted in Sassoon's poetry we hear a double sensitivity, a keening not just for the deaths, but his emotional and erotic love for men, and his own internal conflict when, as 'Mad Jack', he too went out into the wet Flanders night to kill.

In Sassoon's poetry, the dead are drawn just as vividly as the living, tangible ghosts that appear in text with tender intimacy. There's even something erotic about the intensity of Sassoon's desperation for the return of Tommy, the man he loves, in the electric fantasy of the possibility of an adored body returning from the great hereafter to flesh. He writes in 'Invocation', 'come down from heaven's bright hill, my song's desire'. This depth of feeling for the fragility of the male body sits not just in Sassoon's emotional and erotic love for David Thomas, but in the violence he describes throughout his poetry and prose.

Sassoon wrote 'Autumn' at Craiglockhart, a Scottish psychiatric hospital to which he'd been sent in July 1917 after his disgust at the pointless horror of the war had reached a moment of crisis. On 5 June, he wrote a statement condemning the 'war of aggression and conquest' and 'callous complacency' of civilians and politicians, safe back in Blighty, who had no concept of what their sons, husbands, brothers and lovers at the front were having to endure. The short text, which Sassoon called 'A Soldier's Declaration', was read out in Parliament and, rather than face the embarrassment of a public court martial, the military authorities declared him mentally unfit for service and sent him to be treated for shell shock. As the trees around the Craiglockhart estate began to turn, Sassoon thought of the men whom he had led into battle and left behind on the Western Front. He wrote the final anguished couplet of 'Autumn', an acknowledgement of his own complicity in the slaughter: 'O martyred youth and manhood overthrown / The burden of your wrongs is on my head'.

Every night for over a century, a lone bugler has played the Last Post in Ypres. He does so at the Menin Gate that straddles the road Nash painted in 1918, a few kilometres from Sanctuary Wood. The stonework of what Sassoon called a 'sepulchre of crime' is inscribed with 54,889 names of men who died in the battle that destroyed the town, but whose bodies were never found. The ceremony was the final excursion of our battlefields tour. On that evening in the mid '90s the gate's Portland stone and ornamental carved lions glowed in the lights of cafés and bars. We huddled awkwardly in the nippy October air as the note of the brass cut through the quiet murmur of streets to which this had all become familiar. As my memory has it, someone got awkward giggles at the stamping to attention, saluting and formalities, as tends to happen with teenagers at serious moments, and the gravitas was slightly lost as we tried to suppress their contagion. Perhaps, unconsciously, we were in tune with the cynicism of Sassoon's poem about the monument to 'the unheroic Dead who fed the guns'. Militaristic pomp meant little to us, a generation raised in peace, at home if not abroad. Decades of societal change meant the formalities of early twentieth century England seemed as if they were the arcane rituals of another world. We'd not feel a stirring at a song like 'Hearts of Oak'. Now I look back and see our light-heartedness had a poignancy, for a freedom to find ceremony absurd came with our freedom as young men in a peaceful time and place, where we would not have to leave our loved ones to fight and tire and be ground down by modern war for nothing.

In my twenty-something autumns since, the memory of the 1914–18 conflict has become strangely warped by endless arguments over poppies and the 'War Christmas' competitiveness of front gardens made up to look like the trenches. In the mid 1990s, Sanctuary Wood might have been a simulacrum of what had once taken place there, but it was certainly a more realistic and more thoughtful memorial than a suburban driveway complete with LED light explosions and a cardboard cut-out Tommy. A war beyond living memory has been hijacked by a jingoism and nativism that wouldn't have occurred to our naive teenage minds as the breath of our stifled laughter condensed in the chilly air of the damp flatlands of autumn in a small town in northern Europe. Out in the darkness of Sanctuary Wood, dew settled on the broken tree stump, condensing to trickle down into the Flanders soil, where dead roots still mingle with steel and shattered bone.

Equinox: The Open Gate

Anita Roy

21 September 2020. 7.08am.

I turn off the radio stopping the grim newsreader mid-sentence. I can't bear any more statistics. I lace up my walking boots and put on a jacket, head full of graphs and scales and tipping points. I need to get to the Field.

As I leave the pavements behind, the sky lightens and the mist begins to lift. Today promises to be one of those glorious, muted-trumpet days, the Blackdown Hills unfurling against a royal blue backdrop like a heraldic flag, embroidered in gold and beige. One of those days when autumn just wins hands down. Spring with her shy blossoms, summer all lazy and gorgeous, stern-faced winter with ice-chips for eyes – they don't stand a chance.

Autumn on a day like this is a full-body experience. The lane is thick with fallen leaves and they look like they feel – crisp and biscuity; and they sound like they smell – like crushed chestnuts and bonfire smoke. It's a nostalgic hit to all five senses, sending me reeling back until I am a child again, a little girl in a scratchy duffel coat with mittens on a ribbon threaded through the arms, in a body that has only experienced four or five circuits of our nearest star.

Over the stile, the footpath leads straight across a farmer's field where, until a few weeks back, maize had towered over my head, blocking out the view. Now, rows of dry stalks stretch away from my mud-caked boots to vanishing points along the brow of the hill: corn-soldiers slain in a poppyless field. I'm heading due west with the sun at my back, walking into my elongated shadow as though my shadow-self is leading me on. Falling into an easy rhythm – left-right, left-right – literally setting my own pace – walking like this lulls and awakens simultaneously. I wonder if that's why hypnotists use a swinging watch ... a pendulum ... a metronome. Something about the regular rhythm allows the mind to slip the reins, lower the defences, and let strange thoughts arise unbidden.

Ṛtm and *satyam* – Sanskrit words both translatable as 'truth', but whereas *satyam* is expressible and is personal ('my truth'), the truth of *ṛtm* refers to the underlying order of things: it is impersonal and cannot be spoken about.*
Ṛtm is etymologically linked to the English word 'rhythm', and I find myself wondering about the beat – of the heart or of the earth, those anagrammed twins; the seasons' annual boom and bust; the circling earth, the breathing in and out, in and out, left-right, left-right ...

I trudge on up the slope towards the woods, and in my vaguely dissociated state of mind it feels as though it's me that's causing the planet to turn on its axis. Each step does not so much propel me forward as push the Earth back:

---

* Thanks to Ranju Roy for the insights into Sanskrit terminology.

I feel like a very small hamster on a very large wheel, dialling up the sun.

By the time I reach the beech woods, I'm sweating. I take off my jacket, tie it around my waist and carry on. There's an elderly white man out walking his elderly black Labrador coming towards me on the path. 'Oof! Proper Indian summer, we're having, eh?' he remarks as we execute a polite swerve around each other.

It's a phrase whose true meaning I only came to understand embarrassingly recently. You see, I always thought it just meant 'hot' – as in, 'Gosh, isn't the weather hot – you know like in *India*?' But in England, an 'Indian summer' refers to a burst of late warm weather after the summer is over; a few blessed days when the T-shirts and shorts that you'd put away for winter are dug out again, and the skin sucks up solar rays as though they were the last delicious dregs of milkshake from a glass. In India, though, where I lived for twenty years, September is the cruellest month. By the end of August, the monsoon is over, and any cooling effect from the rain has leached away, leaving the air fat with humidity. It's a time of year when every pore is longing for the cool which should – by rights – be exactly where you're headed, but then the mercury starts to rise. Again. You're kind of aghast and indignant. It just doesn't seem fair. You've lived through another Delhi summer, where temperatures can touch 46°C and stay there for days on end, dipping at night-time only to the high thirties. Where you can scald your skin by accidentally touching a car that's been parked in the sun, where people cover their heads and scurry from shady patch to shady patch and life is impossible away from a fan. And after months and months (for those who can afford it – and wimps like me) locked in a deranged love-hate relationship with your air conditioner, there's such a yearning for the cool kiss of winter that watching the September temperatures start to climb again is sheer agony. I remember lying on the stone floor in the bathroom of my flat, the water in the cold tap gushing out hot, thinking, 'But summer is *over*, it's *done*, why the *fuck* is it so hot *again*, this *should not* be happening.' The British September uptick of an 'Indian summer' in actual India is less of a bonus than a sting in the tail.

It's heavenly in these dappled woods, though, and with every fibre of my being I thank my lucky stars that these days my Septembers are spent far from the madding crowds of Delhi (pop. 30 million) and close to the little Somerset town of Wellington (pop. 14,500). Begging Wordsworth's pardon, but bliss it was in that mid-morning to be alive, and to wander among two-hundred-year-old beeches with only the occasional wren, robin, or flittering tag-team of long-tailed tits for company was very heaven.

The Field is still a way off, and I sit on one of the massive low branches to catch my breath. Field with a capital F, you say? Oh yes. She's special, this one. She's something else.

The Field belongs to a friend of mine, a maverick man, a Somerset shaman of sorts, a recluse, a man who has long given up on humans – trusts them about as far as he could throw them – and gone over to the green side. Formidably built and with a stubborn ox-like work ethic, he bought the Field as an exhausted, arid, agricultural plot seventeen years ago. The soil was thin and toxic from years of hard labour under a regime of pesticides and chemical fertilisers. Here he planted three thousand trees, built himself a little shed, wove a toilet out of willow, rigged up a rainwater harvesting system and let the field recover. Today, it is — sorry 'she' is, because, as he told me, 'she's always a she' — a shining example of how nature can bounce back, even from the most shameful abuse. A meadow of wildflowers — vetch and bird's-foot trefoil, primroses, cowslips, orchids and so many different species of wild grasses — in the warm weather alive with insect life, edged by a dense woodland of coppiced hazel, willow and hornbeam, poplar and alder. And somewhere tucked in behind the twisting pathways through the trees, like a witch's cottage in the heart of the wood, the Shed. If you arrive and there's woodsmoke puffing from the tin stovepipe that pokes through the roof, you'll know my friend is there and there's another human hereabouts. But usually — almost always — the Field is left for her other denizens: fox and crow, owl and woodpecker, pheasant and finch, deer and badger and mole.

I'm almost there — another half-hour's hike at most.

My last visit to the Field was the other side of the year — just after the spring equinox, in fact. I'd driven up in the car that time. My heart-rate was up and the pressure of the seatbelt seemed to amplify the thump-thump of my blood. The lockdown – or what we refer to now as 'the first lockdown' – had just been announced, and everyone had that stiff, startled look in their eyes. We all felt like extras in a disaster movie: nobody told us it was going to be that kind of film. On the news, we'd watched an old lady sitting outside a hospital in Spain, wailing. Her husband had just died of Covid, alone and bewildered, attended by exhausted doctors behind their protective shields of plastic. She had tested positive, too. She kept clawing her flimsy mask off, and her son kept gently trying to replace it, as though it could somehow soothe her grief. 'Please don't come to hospital,' a doctor was pleading. 'We cannot cope.' I turned off the news, unable to process what was going on.

You weren't allowed out, but I got in the car all the same. I drove along the empty streets praying I wouldn't be stopped, rehearsing my plea bargain: 'Sorry, officer. I am freaking out and I urgently need to sit in a field.'

I made it to the Field without incident and parked on the grassy verge near the gate. I have a key – my very own key to the Field – which is (in case the caps didn't give it away) a Very Big Deal. It's a mark of trust, not lightly given, and not easily earned – but with this, I feel that the Field is 'mine' – not in any legal or formal sense, but that I have joined the small band of guardians to whom she has been entrusted.

That spring day, not long after the vernal equinox, I sat on my own in the farthest corner, and listened. The M5 lay silent. No rumble of airplanes – not a single white scar in the clear blue sky, a sky that is normally crisscrossed by contrails, up to twenty at a time. It felt as if the whole human world was holding its breath. I sat in the epicentre of a precious, precarious, unprecedented stillness – the like of which I have never experienced in my modern, racing, noisy life – and wondered if this was what it sounded like, nature coming back into its own.

The Field spread around me, or rather, I watched from the wings while she got on with her life. This is one of the very few places on Earth where the balance is right. It's not wild – not really – but neither is it cultivated. The trees have been planted by a human, and their forms altered by his coppicing and trimming, feathering up the lower layers. The grass gets cut using a tractor. The timber is chopped for logs, and smaller branches and twigs are fed through the noisy shredder. There's a grove marked out by slender branches of willow woven at waist-height around it. There's no shortage of signs of human activity – but all this is poised, counterposed, or rather harmonised with the natural ebbs and flows, urges and surges of nature. The wild-flowers have not been selected and sown, but allowed to emerge from the fallow soil.

Spring is a time of beginnings, but that March day, despite the daffodils, despite the primroses, despite the lambs baaing in the field next door, it felt like the end. Nobody seemed to know anything: free-floating anxiety moved across the land like a new trade wind, buffeting us with sudden gusts and temporary lulls. Nauseous with vertigo, I sat there trying to lengthen my out-breath, coaxing my body to relax, to just calm the fuck down. Earthed, I let the electric anxiety leak away into the ground beneath me. The spring sun cupped a hand to my cheek, and I lay against it, giving myself to its healing warmth. After a while, I lay down in the grass, and curled my legs to my chest, ear pressed to the ground as though listening for the *rtm* to rhyme with my own pumping blood, and I fell into a deep sleep. If there was a prayer, it would have been: heal me. Heal us. As you, Our Lady of the Field, have healed yourself. Bring us back to health, as you have brought yourself back to life. Forgive us our terrible, terrible trespasses upon your dear and ancient soil. Deliver us from our insanity, and give us this day a chance to do things differently.

That was then. But this is now: I'm awake and alive (still), and it's the day of the autumnal equinox, and I'm walking along the lane leading to the Field. Have I already missed it? I wonder. Not the gate (although it's so well camouflaged, I often have): I mean the exact moment of equal darkness and light at this point on the Earth's surface. I wasn't sure: did it happen at midnight, or midday? Surely such a momentous moment should be marked – given a countdown, or greeted by fireworks. If ever there were a symbol of our interdependence, the profound connectedness of all us earthlings, it must be this perfectly balanced day when, every six months, everyone everywhere is in the same diurnal boat.

Many people mistakenly think that the seasons happen because of our distance from the sun. That summer is warmer because we're closer, and that the midwinter solstice happens when we're farthest away. In fact, our planet's orbit of the sun is almost exactly circular – at our closest we're about 147 million kilometres away and we never stray more than 152 million kilometres which, in astrological terms, is as near as makes no odds to the strength of the sun's rays on our planet's surface. The seasonal variation in weather is in fact entirely to do with the earth's tilt: 23.5 degrees from the vertical (or, to be precise – and because out in space it's all relative, and there *are* no straight lines in nature – from the plane circumscribed by the earth's orbit around the sun). If there were no tilt, and the earth spun straight, every day would be an equinox: twelve hours of daylight and twelve hours of darkness all the year round – like Venus, in fact, which has no tilt and a roughly circular orbit like our own. It would be hotter and colder, according to latitude, but there'd be no spring, no winter, no monsoon, no hibernation, no first flowerings, no deciduous leaf-shed, no life cycle as we commonly understand it.

Life on Earth was kick-started approximately four and a half billion years ago when our planet collided with a Mars-sized planetoid named, rather poetically, Theia, after the Greek Titaness who was the mother of Helios (the sun), Selene (the moon) and Eos (the dawn). This collision not only knocked Earth off-kilter, it simultaneously sent a smaller chunk of rock orbiting around us, which stabilised the tilt. In other words, it may have been Theia that first set us spinning at 23.5 degrees, but it is her daughter, the moon, whose gravitational pull keeps us there.

We commonly imagine the sun to be a fixed point and that the planets of our solar system orbit around it at lesser or greater distances, but forget (because it's enough to make your head spin) that the sun is moving too – at a rate of 200 kilometres per second, on a circuit of the Milky Way that takes 230 million years to complete. Or to put it another way, as astrophysicist Ethan Siegal so neatly does in *Forbes* magazine: 'Here we are, on planet Earth, which spins on its axis and revolves around the Sun, which orbits in an ellipse around the center of the Milky Way, which is being pulled towards Andromeda within our local group, which is being pushed around inside our cosmic supercluster, Laniakea, by galactic groups, clusters, and cosmic voids, which itself lies in the KBC void amidst the large-scale structure of the Universe.'

I arrive at the Field.

The gate is open.

The gate is *never* open.

My friend has impressed upon me, several times, and quite warmly, that the gate must be shut and the bolt shot home once you enter. And when you leave, you make sure that the chain is in place and the heavy steel padlock is locked. He's a stickler for privacy, this man, and not above chasing out intruders with a large stick.

But today it is wide open, and looks deliberately so, so I leave it there and walk in.

The pathway bends and turns, with trees on either side, so it feels far longer than it actually is. At the end, you emerge onto a wide expanse of grassland which, with the curvature of the hill, feels much bigger than it is too. I always half-expect majestic herds of – I'm not sure, buffalo? wildebeest? – to be roaming across it, and yet it's only two acres across and bounded on three sides by ploughed agricultural fields or sheep pasture, and is (at least on paper) as tame a piece of real estate as you could get.

The sun feels closer – the back of my head feels lightly toasted – as I make my way through this wild and gardened meadowscape and into the woodland labyrinth. Sure enough, the shed is puffing its pipe, and my friend greets me with a wave as I emerge into the clearing.

Strictly speaking, it's against the rules, but we risk a hug. I stand in his bearlike embrace, wringing every last ounce of tactile nourishment from the closeness of another breathing, warm human creature to see me through the next weeks or months or years – who knows? – of arid social distancing, jokey elbow clonks, hug-gestures mimed at masked friends across the street, and the ubiquitous Zoom-zoo boxed off from each other in our little square cages.

'How come the gate's open?' I say, when we've stopped hugging and exchanged the usual (although these days far more pointed) 'how-are-yous'?

'I left it open for all the souls,' he says, and I immediately get it.

You see, my friend has form. Apart from being a plant whisperer, master propagator, and something of a ragged-trousered misanthropist, he helps people 'across'. There's a reason that I call him a shaman, and it's not only to do with his preference for animals over humans, or his unorthodox views on the animating spirits of the natural world, or even for the place where he lives (actually and symbolically) on the outskirts of civilisation. It's because of his experience with helping dying people to die, of holding the door open – as he puts it – into the other world.

When I fled to the Field in the spring, I was pursued by general anxiety fuelled by the news of the pandemic and accelerated by upward spiking graphs. Alarming, horrifying, overwhelming as these were, you'd have thought by now we'd be used to it, given the similar infographics on climate change. But alongside this, in the early days of the pandemic was a very specific fear to do with not only the sheer number of people dying, but in this new, modern, and very specific way: isolated, alone, intubated, surrounded by nurses and doctors in PPE, unable to touch or be touched, bewildered and afraid. I was terrified for my father and my mum (aged ninety-four and eighty respectively) – and still am – and grief-stricken for all those thousands of families who have had to endure this additional horror. By the autumnal equinox, the number of deaths in the UK is fast approaching 50,000. All those lost souls, all that restless turmoil – and winter on the horizon.

'It's heartbreaking, it really is,' says my friend. And for a man who so roundly and routinely decries the human race, he sounds suspiciously like someone who cares.

'I've helped quite a few across in my time,' he says, eyeing me sideways, daring me to disbelieve. 'I got quite known for it, back then.' He makes a delicate gesture with his heavy workman's hands, as though sprinkling something from his fingers. 'It's a gift.'

He reaches over to pour a bit more coffee into my mug, and we settle back in our fold-out fisherman's chairs, at a sensible distance. 'I don't do that much any more,' he goes on, 'but I couldn't stand to see so many troubled souls, so left the gate open so's they know. They're welcome here. They can come here and rest, find some peace maybe.'

I like that. I know it's where I'd like to come, in the unlikely event you get a choice in the matter when you're done with the bodily part of your existence. It's becoming something of a launchpad for departing souls, this Field. My friend is already nurturing the tree he's intending to go under – it even has a name (Freddy) and seems to be quite happy growing away as it waits for him to catch up. And in the meadow, there's a circle of newly planted willow whips jutting out of the miscanthus grass margins along one side, with an acer in the middle, where another friend's ashes are scattered. When my uncle – my father's brother – died in India, we held a small family ceremony for him up at the Field. My brother and sister-in-law chanted Sanskrit shlokas to speed him on his way. We burnt incense, told stories and offered sweets and fresh fruit. We drank gingery chai and joked that there was a corner of this Somerset field that was forever – or for a little while anyway – India.

My friend finishes his coffee and stands up, scattering the dregs into the grass, and I do the same.

'Well,' I say, 'best be off.'

'Right you are. Take care, then.'

'You too.'

'Leave the gate open as you go.'

And I do.

The afternoon rolls on, radiant, the last great chord of a symphony in the sweet reprieve of an Indian summer's day in late English September. As I walk back home, the beeches let their golden pennies drop, and I remember my friend asking me why it is that leaves in autumn fall – or rather, why a single leaf falls at a particular moment. Before I could embark on an explanation of photosynthesis, photoperiodicity in plants and vegetal dormancy, he stopped me with one of his infuriating Somerset koans: 'Is it the tree that drops the leaf, or the leaf that decides to let go?'

Tree? Leaf? Wind? Stalk? Where does one end or the other begin? Humans! So busy trying to make sense of things, so good at not trusting what their senses *do* say. I give up trying to quieten my metaphor-making monkey mind. All those imaginary lines, axes and degrees, angles of rotation, of incidence and reflection, of tipping points and see-saw seasons, of life and death, summer and winter, future and past, and the impossible task of pinning down where is 'here' or when is 'now'.

Look. There I am, putting one foot in front of the other, heading down into the valley – and above me, a skyful of bewildered souls, rising up from the horizon and wheeling towards the Field, like a flock of pigeons, homing.

It's Hopping Time

Raine Geoghegan

Covels packed
chavies scrubbed clean
me rackley's bal
washed with panni
the grai grizhomed, holled.

(*Romany words, or 'jib':* covels – belongings; chavies –
children; rackley – girl; grai – horses; grizhomed –
groomed; holled – fed)

I have moved back to the borders of Herefordshire and Worcestershire, the place to where my Romany family and ancestors used to travel each year to pick fruit, vegetables and hops. I live near to the hop fields in Bishop's Frome and it was here that my ancestors picked hops for hundreds of years. It's also the place where my mother met my father and so it seems rather fitting to be based here now. For the last couple of years I have been writing poems, monologues and songs about my Romany family as a way to reconnect with them, especially those I can't remember or never knew. I hold my ancestors close in my mind and they accompany me on my journeys through geographies of memory. Autumn, the season of balance, of turning inwards and breathing a sigh of relief as the heat of the summer wanes. What gifts are we given at this time of the year? I will name some of mine. Light, the way it falls across the land and transfigures everything; the harvest, season of abundance, apples, pears, plums, falling ripe into our hands; trees, the leaves changing colour, from shades of green to burnished copper, crimson, purple hues and full-throated oranges and pinks; the myth and magic of the season encouraging us to practise simple rituals and give thanks for the abundance of the land.

It's September, my favourite month, when the earth is soft and yielding. I have travelled from West Sussex to Gloucestershire and am now here on the borderland. Whenever I travel anywhere I think of my Romany ancestors who used to travel along the roads with their vardos and grai, wagons and horses. The poem which begins this chapter is a typical scenario of the start of a Traveller woman's preparation for a journey. I think of how they would travel in a vardo with the horses up front, how they'd move slowly along the roads. How would I cope with that sort of life? I'm not sure but I like to commemorate those travelling people through my writing. I'm not a fan of the speed with which cars travel on the road and I like to take several breaks wherever I am going, to pause, have a cup of tea, to stretch my legs. I love that whole 'Slow Movement' in Italy, whereby in some of the towns there is a law that states drivers are not allowed to go above a certain speed. It derives from the 'Cittaslow Movement' which is about improving the quality of life in cities by promoting a slower lifestyle. The aim is to reduce stress and improve health. My husband gets frustrated with me but even he at times enjoys this way of travelling.

Autumn is a time of boundaries. We are approaching the Celtic New Year and there is that sense of otherness in the air. I now live on the border of two counties as well as being in that liminal place between Wales, my birthplace, and England. As we move towards the threshold of ripeness and death I am reminded of my father's passing on 14 September and the fact that it is a month that I love. I am aware of the energy of this season shifting from active mode to that of slowing down and reflecting on the busyness of summer. I begin to let go of my burdens. Like the leaves that will start to fall, I too must let go. I am already aware of how the weather affects my body. I have fibromyalgia and arthritis, which always worsen at this time. Come the end of autumn I will be hibernating just like a hedgehog. As a child I lived with my Romany grandparents. My granny had arthritis in her hands. She sold flowers and wore fingerless gloves but she never moaned about the pain or the cold. My memories of autumn are my granny dressed in her thick coat, wearing ankle boots and a woollen hat, fixed tight on her head with a large gold hatpin. She would bring the flowers into the house from the shed, place them in black buckets filled with water in the hallway. In the morning when I came down for breakfast, I would smell the strong scents of chrysanthemums and carnations. At night my grandfather would light a fire and sit in front of it, often roasting chestnuts or toasting bread and warming his hands. My mother would make meat and plum puddings, cooked in a cloth in a pot. She would tell me about her grandparents and how she'd visit them in Shepperton.

The Plum Pudding Girl

'Phylly put yer chockas on.
It's time to go to Shepperton,
to see yer gran and grandad
on a windy Friday night.
Plum pudden,
meat pudden,
bacon pudden,
suet pudden,
cooked in a cloth, tied with a string.
You'll 'ave to sing a song fer them
and do a little dance fer them
then they will blow the joter
when the 'obben's in the pot.'

(chockas – shoes; joter – whistle; 'obben – food)

I think about my granny's stories of living in a vardo. When my mother was a few months old she contracted pneumonia. A doctor was called and there wasn't much he could do. My great-aunt made up a poultice by crushing comfrey and mustard seeds into a paste. This was placed on the baby's chest and then the long night saw the family sitting up, drinking tea and praying for her recovery. My Romany family used the gifts of Nature for all of their ailments. Wild garlic, brimstone, coltsfoot and dandelion were just some of the herbs used. Wherever they found themselves, they would know what to pick and always by instinct. We have lost this knowledge and I mourn it considerably. Thankfully, the poultice worked and my dear mother lived until she was sixty-three.

I believe that my own relationship to Nature has been greatly influenced by my Romany family. I have a natural affinity with the land, the trees, mountains and water. Connecting with Nature is a way of acknowledging and honouring all that is around us. I call my relationship with Nature 'Deep Living', and what this means to me is that I honour my path on the earth. I am mindful of my footfall and what I do every day. I witness the beauty that is around me but I also witness the destruction and the self-centred needs of many people. Perhaps this idea of 'Deep Living' was one of the gifts I received when I was bedbound with severe ME/Chronic Fatigue Syndrome at the age of forty. I spent long, difficult days unable to do the basic things; even washing my hair was so challenging that my husband used to do it for me. I saw the seasons change through my bedroom window but I remember that one September afternoon I sat in the garden. I had begun to keep a journal and was writing short pieces every day. It helped me to keep track of the days and my illness. I remember how the sun warmed me and I felt a glimmer of hope, a sense that I would get better but I may have to wait a while. Since then, September has been my favourite month. My life has been defined in a new way by illness and disability. I rest in the mornings and I take my time to do each task. I see more of what is around me, noticing the little things: the sky changing colour; a blackbird swooping onto the lawn and pecking at the grass; the way the moon glows in the night sky; small wildflowers bursting through a crack in the pavement. For me, everything comes back to Nature. I look upon her as a mirror and I see the reflection of who I am, or who I want to be. Nature is a spiritual pathway, a guide, a healing presence. I know this was true for my Romany ancestors. They may have lived in vardos but the wild fields and pathways were their home. In the summer months they would often sleep outside and in the autumn they would go hopping. They were called 'tardra-mengre' – hop-pickers.

Hop-picking season began in early September. In the latter years my family would pick hops in Bishop's Frome, Herefordshire, but there were times in the early days that they would go to Paddock's Wood in Kent. Three or four families would travel together and there would be much preparation as well as a growing sense of excitement, especially from the children. These are the sort of events that would remain in a child's memory.

Koring Chiriclo II – a triolet

Jel on, me dad would say.
Pack up yer covels; we'll be on our way.
Take our time; get to Frome's Hill by May.

Jel on, me dad would say.
The cuckoo's callin', untie the grai,
up onto the vardo. It's a kushti day.
Jel on, me dad would say.
Pack up yer covels. We'll be on our way.

(Koring Chiriclo – the cuckoo; jel on – move on; covels –
belongings; grai – horses; vardo – wagon; kushti – lovely)

Frome's Hill lies close to Bishop's Frome, only a few miles
from where I'm living now. It's a small hamlet high on the
hill and when I drive there on my way to the hop fields I
never fail to be surprised by the glorious view of the rich
Herefordshire countryside and the Welsh hills in the
distance. I was born in the Welsh valleys, a place of contrasts
but also a place where my soul feels the *hiraeth*, that deep
sense of longing for home. The Hop Pocket, a large retail
store and café, was built on the site of the hop fields and it's
a regular haunt of mine. I like to stroll around the building
and look out at the hop fields, which are still there. I imagine my family picking the hops, their bodies bent over, hard
at it but always making the time to have a laugh or to sing
a song. My mother's cousin, Shirley Reece, told me a story
about how my grandmother, Amy Lane, once laid a table in
the middle of a hop field, just as she would have done in
her own home. Shirley said that it was a very funny sight. I
loved the story so much that I wrote a poem about it.

The Table in the Hop Fields,
Bishop's Frome, Shirley's tale

We got to the 'op fields just as the sun was coming up. We walked across the poove and there was our Aunt Amy, pouring panni from the kettle into the big brown teapot. She'd covered the table with a white lace cloth and 'ad laid out 'er best china crockery.

'Ere you are my gels, come and 'ave a bit of breakfast and a nice cup of mesci.'

Me sister and I couldn't 'elp but laugh, the table looked so funny in the middle of nowhere.

'Now listen 'ere, we got a pick a lot of 'ops today, yearn ourselves some poshes.'

We had to sit on a red checked blanket, the grass still wet from the morning dew. She gave us bread, cheese and a cup of sweet mesci. We looked up at all the 'obben that she'd prepared for the 'oppers. Plates of bread and ham, cheese, pickles and funny shaped biscuits. She put 'er 'ands on 'er 'ips and looked around as if she was waiting for someone.

'Ere 'ee is, 'bout time too.' It was our Uncle Tommy, come all the way from Anarth; I knew wiv 'im 'elpin' we'd pick loads of 'ops.

'Ee came stridin' across the poove, a big smile on 'is face, 'is trilby on and 'is waistcoat all buttoned up, 'ee always did look smart.

'Well well, ain't this kushti Amy? Yer made yerself at 'ome, I see. What a luvley spread'.

'It don't seem that long ago that we were on rations Tom

and you know me I do like a nice bit of grub.'

'Ee kissed 'er cheek, bent down, tickled us gels and made us giggle. One by one the rest of our people joined us, wanting breakfast. They were just as amused at the sight of the table as me sister and me. We all knew that Aunt Amy liked to do 'er own thing, we never knew what the next thing might be.

hungry finches
waiting for crumbs
as we ate our grub
a bell rings
it's hopping time

(Poove – field; panni – water; mesci – tea;
poshes – money; hobben – food; kushti – very nice)

In the 1980s I recorded my grandmother's voice as she told me about her hop-picking days. I wanted to capture some of her stories while she was alive. I still have this recording of the oral testimonies that she made.

We never 'ad a lot money, so we 'ad to work 'ard in the fields. Monday mornin' we were up early, we got ready then out in the 'op yards we went. Me grandfather said to me 'Ame, pick that basket up.' It 'ad all the cups and saucers in it, a cloth laid over the top and I put it over me arm, the kittle over me other arm, then off we went. It was cold in the mornings, we 'ad to put layers on and thick socks but we soon warmed up. I was a dirty picker, the leaves going everywhere but my Alf, 'ee was a clean picker. Ooh, 'ee we did work 'ard but then at night we used to go to the Green Dragon, all the men 'ad a lift in the cart and the women followed on. The landlord used to fill up a bath and pour the beer into it for the 'oppers. Ooh we did 'ave a good time, singin', dancin', tellin' stories, yer can't beat it.

The hop fields of Bishop's Frome are also the place where my mother met my father. He had travelled from the Welsh Valleys with his friends, not wanting to go into the coal mines, and they would pick fruit and hops wherever they could. He fell in love with my mother. She too loved the autumn, 'tamna' in the Romany jib, and I think it's because she was so happy in the fields, surrounded by the stunning countryside of Herefordshire and the fact that there was a real sense of community and friendship. She loved this county, as I do.

Kamavtu

Mother was from Middlesex,
father, the Welsh Valleys.
He was a pole puller, she picked the hops.

One Friday night
under a sickle of moonlight
they sat on a bench
in front of the Green Dragon pub.

The landlord had filled an old bath with beer,
the hoppers were dipping their mugs into the frothy
     liquid,
which dripped onto their bare chests.

They were smiling as they wiped their mouths on the
     backs of their arms.

Father and Mother sat quietly holding hands.
He leaned in close, was about to kiss her cheek
when a voice hollered from the darkness.

'Phylly, jel on, let's get back to the vardo.'
'It's me dad,' she said.

She jumped up, straightening her long skirt
then quickly turned and whispered,

'Kamavtu Jimmy.'

He didn't know many Romany words but this one, well
     he just knew.
          (Kamavtu – Romany word for 'I love you')

Here is another testimony from my grandmother, talking
about being paid by the busheler.

At the end of the day, we'd all straighten our backs and get
ready for the busheler. He came round and weighed the

'ops then 'ee'd pay us. 42 bushel I 'ad cut, me dad laughed all over 'is face. I beat all the lot, my Raine. So now we done six weeks pickin' an' I yearned, well me and Alf yearned over £200. Me dad looked at me and he said, 'Ame, I lost a good picker when you went to work with Alf.' I cried.

Autumn was indeed a time of plenty for my Romany family. I recently met up again with my mum's cousin, Shirley, and she had this to say:

I was a small child but I remember it well. The excitement of getting ready and leaving Middlesex. We didn't have wagons then, not like in the past. We would travel to Herefordshire in lorries and vans. I remember staying in small huts, the cooking was done outside, the pots hung on kettle hooks. Our mums made meat and bacon pudden. Sometimes they cooked a hock of bacon or shushi (rabbit). We were all given bales of straw to make up our beds and a sack of potatoes. The farmer also gave us oil and a tin fire called the 'hop-devil'. September time could be chilly. It was hard work and we children did our best but our hands used to smell of sulphur and sting from picking hops. They smelled sweet. We liked the night times, the singing and storytelling.

As I reflected on Shirley's story and imagined the scene I came up with the following prose poem.

Hobben Time in the Hop-Picking Days

Once a week we'd bake an 'edghog, roll it in clay, bake it in
the embers of the yog then leave it for a good while and
break open the clay. The chavvies liked to watch this but
there was always one who cried, feeling sorry for the little
creature. Well we 'ad to eat. We ate a lot of stew, especially
if it was a cold or damp day. Us Romanies used to pick all
our own vegetables in exchange for doin' a bit of work for
the farmers. The men would bring 'ome the odd pheasant
and we'd pick fresh 'erbs. We liked a lot of salt 'n' pepper.
Kushti. Afterwards we drank strong mesci, none of this
wishy-washy stuff that they make nowadays. I liked to put
a drop of whiskey in it, a lot of us did, but there were a few
who didn't touch the stuff. Me Aunt Louie wouldn't drink,
she said it was the devil's brew and if yer drank it, you'll go
didilow.

(Chavvies – children; kushti – lovely; didilow – mad)

Apples

As well as hop-picking my family used to pick fruit and
other vegetables in Kent, Worcestershire and Herefordshire.
They would move from farm to farm throughout the
summer picking cherries, strawberries, peas and beans
before going on to pick hops, potatoes and apples in the
autumn. Potato-picking was the last thing they did before
settling down in the winter. After that they would make
pegs, paper and wooden flowers and sell clothes (togs). The

Vale of Evesham was a popular apple-picking area and my grandparents used to pick apples there. I heard many stories of those times and again I have put pen to paper to try and capture one of those moments.

Apple Picking Days in the Vale of Evesham

You're in the orchard,
sitting on the grass
with the woody scent of apples and earth,
a basket full of Worcester Pearmans at your feet.
You take the smallest one,
wipe it on your purple apron,
lean your head back to catch the sun.
'Ere you are my gel, a kushti slice of apple.'
Four years old again and daddy is cutting the fruit,
slicing it with his special little churi,
the one his father gave him.
He grins as the juice dribbles down your chin.
One hand on your belly
you feel the baby kick,
you take another bite,
watch your husband in the tree,
his strong hands pulling the fruit
from the branches
taking one from the right
another from the left
dropping them into the straw basket
which hangs low around his neck

'Not long to go now.'
He climbs down the ladder
drops his load onto the soft earth
stretches his arms wide.
'Yer done now, Alf?'
'Yes, my love.'
Fifty years later
as you wave goodbye to your granddaughter,
you remember,
the baby kicking,
Alf in the tree,
autumn sunshine
and the strong smell of the Worcesters.

(Kushti – very nice; churi – a small knife)

Nowadays the farmers use specialist picking machines, as I remember when living in Much Marcle last year, close to Weston's Cider. The farmers and their machines would come round at the beginning of autumn and I would watch them through the window. There was an apple orchard right next door to our house. There was also a herd of heifers that had great fun using their long tongues to catch hold of the branches of the apple trees. They would then shake the branches so the apples fell in abundance to the ground. I loved watching them fill their stomachs with the fallen fruit. The first pamphlet that I wrote is called *Apple Water: Povel Panni*. Apple water country, 'povel-panni tem' in the Romany jib, is the name that was given to the county of Herefordshire by the old Gypsies in George Borrow's time. Of course, 'apple water' refers to the cider and it's appropriate as Herefordshire is known as the cider capital. I've always thought that apples are a rather special fruit. I remember my grandfather cutting them in a particular way and showing me the five-tip stars which form a pentagram. Gypsies still cut apples in this way and the apple cores are known as 'stars of knowledge'. In Ireland where my gadje (non-Romany) great-grandparents are from, the concept of the five points is still symbolic as Ireland has five great roads, five provinces and five paths of the law. I am half-Romany and half-gadje, so am known as a 'didikai'. Like my pamphlet I have come back to 'apple water country', the place of my beginning. The name for Kent was hop country, 'tardra tem' in Romany. This idea of naming each county makes sense as the Travellers went from place to place depending on what they were going to pick.

Singing for the Trees

I stop to sit on a log in Priory Park and breathe in the coolness of the air. The late sun is filtering through the leaves, creating shadows and light play. I have a disability. Many years ago I fell down the stairs, damaging my pelvis and in particular my coccyx; that and being bedbound for a number of years with ME/Chronic Fatigue Syndrome means I am unable to walk very far and can't stand for more than a few minutes. It's frustrating but I have learned to sit and observe the beauty that is around me. It's a blessing to be surrounded by so many trees here; there's even a cedar tree, which looks very old. So it is that I sit here for a while and calm my mind as I listen to the sounds of birds and the branches that shake and bend as the breeze dances amongst them. I notice the grand fir trees, how powerful and magnificent they are. All around me I see the oaks, willows, silver birch, spruce and beech trees, all seem to be reaching for the sky. There is a stream nearby and my mind becomes aware of how inter-connected Nature is, the trees, fields, rivers, mountains and the ocean. I find myself singing for the trees, an old song.

The river she is flowing, flowing and growing, the river she is flowing, down to the sea. Oh mother carry me, a child I will always be. Oh mother carry me, down to the sea.

I mention this to a friend of mine. She is a storyteller and she told me about a woman she once met from the Sámi tribe in Norway. The woman practised something called 'yoiking' and she was singing in this way to an old tree in Malvern. My friend was fascinated by the tone and pitch of this type of singing. Yoiking is a traditional form of song that the Sámi people sing in honour of the earth. It's not unlike the songs of the First Nations people but it is often discordant and unlike anything that we know of. I am reminded of some-thing that my grandfather used to do. It was called diddling which is a form of singing that the Romany Travellers, espe-cially the men, have always done. Now I don't know whether or not it was sung in honour of anything in particular but it had a kind of reverence even though, written on the page, it looks like the sort of thing a child would like to sing. It goes like this: 'diddilie dee, diddilie die, diddilie, diddilie do'. I remember my grandfather diddling when he was making small vardos out of wood; perhaps he was honouring the wood as he carved it into shapes? This is an excerpt of a poem that I wrote about just that.

Making the Vardos

Sitting on the doorstep
he picks up his churi,
makes the first cut into the oak,
the finest for small vardos.
He's taken to this since moving into the ken,
he's made one for two of his children,
now he's on the third.
The jook watches him as he carves the door,
he thinks of painting it red,
Mary's best colour.
He works quietly,
dropping the shavings into a bowl.
He remembers making the pegs,
'chinnin' the koshties,' they called it
when he was on the drom.

(Churi – peg knife; vardos – wagons; jook – dog;
chinning the koshties – making the pegs; drom - road)

Making pegs was something my grandfather did and in the autumn he would make a large quantity of them. He and my granny would also make paper and wooden flowers to sell ready for Christmas time. The house was always full of these things and as I look back I am reminded of the productivity that filled our home. My grandparents, mum, sister and I plus the dog all lived together. It was a happy time, apart from not having our dad with us. He had died when I was nineteen months old so I never actually knew him.

There's something about autumn that is conducive to reflection and introspection. Perhaps it's a time when the earth shifts into a gentler gear, where Nature calls us to be attentive, to notice the movements of wind and water and to wake up, open our eyes to the deep beauty that is all around us.

Blackhill

I walk, with the aid of my walking stick, to a clearing on Blackhill in the Malvern Hills. I sit on a bench looking out to the Cotswolds. There are houses dotted in the distance and smoke rising from the chimneys, early fires that have been lit ready for the evening. In front of me are a number of silver birches; the autumn light brings them to life, giving an impression of a stage set. I sit here as if I'm watching a silent movie. I have to rest often as the pain in my back escalates when I walk. I watch people climb the hill. Thankfully, the frustration and sadness that was once so acute has given way to acceptance and the challenge to see the world around me with new eyes. There are still times when I would give anything to be able to walk up the hills without pain. I rise, walk for a short while, then sit down again. All is well. Blackhill is one of my favourite spots as I can see for miles and the sky is never the same from one day to the next. I also sense the landscape here, how it has character and a strong presence. I am surrounded by hills, trees and water that filters through the rock. On my way home I stop and drink from one of the wells in Jubilee Drive. There are many wells here in Malvern and the water is the most delicious I've ever tasted. It has a slight sweetness in terms of flavour and of course is chilled as it comes straight from the ground. How blessed we are to have this rich source of natural water that has been flowing for thousands of years. It truly is a gift and I am so grateful for it. I find that it has a very beneficial effect on me. It wakes me up and connects me with something deep and powerful.

Samhain/Old Souls/Hallowmas
– 31 October/1 November

I sit in front of photographs of my ancestors. I open my mind and reach out to them. I silently thank them for all the gifts they have given me: my life blood; my Romany, Welsh and Irish ancestry; my talents and many other things. I am aware of how the Romany traditions, language and culture are under threat. I do what I can to preserve the language, sometimes speaking it aloud with my family or using it in my poetry. I hope that my children and grandchildren will follow me in keeping it alive. My family didn't follow a religion but they worshipped the land. Some Romany Travellers worship Saint Sara-Kali, the Patron

Saint of Gypsies. I have a photograph of her on my altar and I am reminded of a few lines of a poem that I wrote recently, a reimagining of her:

Man made me into a saint but my life belongs to my race and the days gone past, a time when religion was found in the clay, in the mountains and forests, in the song of the wind and at a mother's breast.

These words remind me of my granny who celebrated each and every day. She lived life fully and was proud of her roots. She tended her garden and loved telling me about her parents and the old days. I read a poem that I wrote in her memory.

A Memory of the Hop Fields

She is in the front garden
bending low, picking bluebells,
wearing her old red apron,
with the Spanish dancer on the front.
She stands up, rubbing her lower back,
her mind shaping a memory,
The hop fields,
her mother lean, strong,
Picking the hops as quick as a squirrel.
Her bal in plaits, tied on top of her head.
Her gold hoops, pulling her ears down.
Ruddy cheeks, dry cracked lips.
Her father pulling poles,

sweating, smiling,

his gold tooth for all to see.

At the end of a long day

she would stand on top of an apple crate,

comb his hair, kiss his neck tasting of salt.

He would pick her up,

swing her high, low and say,

'You're the prettiest little chi there ever was.'

(Bal – hair; chi – daughter/child)

I love the early evenings in autumn. I am sitting by the window and looking out at the mist, which had completely covered Bredon Hill earlier today. I can see the hill now and the sky has turned pale pink. I reflect on my early life before my father died. My mother and he never settled in one place; instead they went back and forth from the Welsh Valleys to a village in Middlesex called Hanworth. My mother preferred England and my father wanted the valleys. Perhaps this is why I have never felt settled anywhere, this and the Gypsy spirit which propels me to seek new pastures. Home for Travellers is something intangible. Whenever they pulled their wagons onto a patch of land, that was their home, and so it is for me. I wonder if I'll still be in Malvern in a few years' time.

I was always taught that it's the simple things that matter. For my ancestors this meant sitting in the autumn sunshine, drinking a cup of mesci (tea), watching the chavies (children) playing and roaming free in the poove (field). They knew the land well, it was their home and they treated it with respect and reverence. A Gypsy knows the importance of the relationship between the sole of the foot and the soul of the earth. Each step they take strengthens their connection to the land. For me, I too love the simple day-to-day activities like watching the ever-changing sky as it makes a kaleidoscope of patterns here in Malvern or looking out at the Herefordshire countryside or just sitting in my garden listening to a blackbird sing. I may not be able to go off hiking but my love of nature heals and empowers me, wherever I am. I see my own divinity in Nature and, in honouring her, I honour myself. As I gaze upon the red sumac and the hazel tree in my garden, I silently say, 'Hello old friends.'

As I come to the end of autumn, and feel the cold snap at my heels, the voices of my ancestors echo through my poetry, they carry me through the darker days of winter. I imagine I am sitting with them around the fire, listening to their stories and songs. Under my feet the earth is moving, preparing for new growth and it won't be long before I see tiny shoots of green and the first snowdrops. For now I give thanks for tamna time and for the gifts which are freely given.

Opre and gel on
dikk the next atchin tan
a fellow chal pookers

(Opre – arise/forward; dikk – look; atchin tan – stopping place;
chal – travelling man pookers – calls out)

The poems in this text are published in my two collections: *Apple Water: Povel Panni* (2018) and *They Lit Fires: Lenti Hatch o Yog* (2019) with Hedgehog Poetry Press.

WINTER

Coming in from the Cold

Zakiya McKenzie

'Mama, tell me what snow is like?' I asked, sitting down
on a beach towel beside my mother one December. My
sister was deep in concentration at my mother's feet,
building a magnificent sandcastle, my dad and brother on
either side of my grandfather in the vast blue water before
us. The waves glistened with sunlight and turned frothy
white as they crashed loudly into rocks at the far end of
the seashore. The sun shone down so ferociously that you
could fall asleep right there in the sand and slumber stead-
ily for hours. 'Sun drunk yuh,' we would say when the
sleeper awoke, because we knew that sprawled beneath an
almond tree on cool sand was sometimes the sweetest
sleep anyone could get – deep and hypnotic, as cleansing
as the seawater itself. You would wake up to fried fish and
festival, or pepper shrimp and warm grotto bread. Or to
Fudgey squeezing his horn alerting you to the icy treats
on the back of his motorcycle or to the excitement of a
security guard who is himself glued to a little radio for
news or, better yet, West Indies cricket match updates.
Always, there would be a sound system near a canteen
playing bass-heavy reggae tunes – this time of year it

would be something like King Yellowman singing a carol about breadfruit roasting on an open fire, and not a chestnut in sight.

'Snow? Snow is like sugar,' my mother answered, laughing. She looked directly in my puzzled eyes and waited for a response. My sister stopped her work and looked up too.

'Sweet?' I asked.

'Sweet in the sense that it's fun to play in, yes.'

'Ma, what you mean? Sugar is brown and grainy ...' my sister jumped in, one hand on hip, bucket and spade in the other.

'Alright, alright,' our mother chuckled while grabbing a handful of sand. 'Our brown sugar is like this, but snow? Snow is like white sugar falling from the sky. You girls want to hear a story about a little girl who went to England from an island just like this one and saw snow for the first time?'

'Yes!' we squealed in unison, cosying up beside Mum the storyteller.

'Eh, crick?' she began the call.

'Eh, crack!' we gave the response.

'Now listen up and listen good; this is a story about moving from one season to the next ...'

1960s
Mother

'Wake up, Petal. Here's a letter from Papa.' It was a thin, blue envelope marked 'Airmail'.

'Papa send money for your passage to London this winter. My baby, how can I live with my baby gone to the cold?'

This is how my mother found out she was moving to England, from my grandmother in rural Jamaica to my grandfather in metropolitan London.

A six-year-old does not know what to expect so she did not expect three months of preparations. Breadfruit was roasted until the skin went from a milky green to charcoal black. Ackee pods needed to ripen and be picked at the right time so that the yellow fruit inside arrived in London intact. Red and blue snapper were fished from the sea and fried, while big stones were lifted in calm parts of the river for janga (crayfish) to swim out into waiting hands. This was regular groundwork for a Jamaican December-time, but most of the measures for this journey to the cold were to do with the weather. My mother recalled that it seemed most of her mother's focus was on making sure her daughter did not freeze to death during the last leg of the journey, from aeroplane to front door. Pusha, the Rasta man who still lives by the bridge down the road, was employed to knit a tam out of purple yarn. Gloves proved a little harder for him to pattern and so she ended up with mittens that were not really mittens at all, but more akin to little woollen drawstring bags for hands. My mother only knew the seasons in Jamaica – being outside every day of the year, Auntie Marva's veranda that turned into a classroom on weekday mornings, Maas Harry's bar piazza that grew rowdier as the sun went to sleep – it was hard to imagine a place where she would need three jackets, a scarf, hat and mittens to be where she loved the most, the great outdoors.

My mother first went to England during one of the coldest winters that country had ever seen. Months and months where the days were inky and the nights were frigid with lonely unfamiliarity that lacked the warmth of a snuggle in her mother's lap. It was colder still to a child who had spent all her life in a place where the sun watched over her every move. That Jamaican countryside sun was her companion; if it was still up there, she could roam wherever her little feet could take her, and she knew that when the day star turned the colour wheels of the sky from blue to orangey-purple, it was time to go home. It was so unlike the place she would come to know that seemed to be grey for weeks at a time. It took my mother a long time to accept the dark season.

My mother arrived in England before she was wrapped in the comfort of Grace Nichols delivering 'Lady Winter's Rap', before she could laugh with Trish Cooke in *Mammy, Sugar Falling Down*. She was born the year Sam Selvon published *The Lonely Londoners*, a novel that so fluidly conjured up the visceral shifts in the lives of Caribbean migrants to the city, spurred on by the cold. So, like the boys in Selvon's novel, 'one grim winter evening, when it had a kind of unrealness about London, with a fog sleeping restlessly over the city and the lights showing in the blur as if is not London at all but some strange place on another planet . . .', my mother arrived in Britain for the first time, and this strange place was to become her home.

On the ride from the airport my mother, a child, marvelled at the lack of blue above, and wondered if there was something wrong with her eyes after being in the air for so many hours. In the new country, the sun held itself back leaving a murky array of shades of black, white and grey. The trees stood naked and stark, empty billboards highlighting the want of more from the colour wheel. My mother did not know that the leaves returned with haste in the spring and she was frightened of the mocking stance from the stems for weeks until she brought up the courage to ask about it. What a shock it was to her, a little country girl who had never even been to the capital city of her birth island. She had only ever known the interior of valleys and the topography of the Eastern Jamaican hillside, forever covered in brawny greens. So strange was it to leave a place where there is no semblance of winter, no understanding of the change in season, which takes place so often in other parts of the world that human beings have learned to live with it. There was no shade to rest under, no canopy to hide beneath and my mother felt really exposed. In her new world, this new season called 'winter' meant a life indoors since the sharp edge of outside air pushed you back towards the warmth inside. On the night she arrived at her London home for the first time, my mother recalled learning that one of the most satisfying moments of any winter is being able to shut your door to it.

On that first night, my mother lay in her new bed, thinking about how even the coldest Christmases were never this cold back home, but the things swirling in her head were interrupted by the heavy front door she had come through a few hours ago opening and closing with a loud crack on the hinge. A deep voice greeted the pretty lady who introduced herself as 'stepmother', but the owner of the voice did not wait for a response. Instead, steady clambering footsteps came up towards the bedroom. As the doorknob turned, my mother sank lower into the bed, one eye peeking over the covers, shocked by the hulking silhouette stepping through the door and towering over her. She tried her best to swallow the cold sobs but she could not help but cry. The figure reached up and pulled on the light switch. This was the tallest man she had ever seen, made even more imposing by the long grey coat, thick neck scarf and brown hat. The man's face softened when their eyes met in the light and she thought she recognised something in it.

'My Petal, it's me,' he said. 'Papa.'

As the years passed by, my mother became more familiar with the frosty winter, even more than the tropical climate and my grandmother, whom she had left in Jamaica. The scary and unknown became the soft and loved in London; winter's appeal grew every time she hugged her stepmother, little sisters and father before jumping into her cosy bed. But, children only remember the best parts and the imagined winter utopia made way for reality's weathering as she got older. It was hard to relate to barren city parks and the loss of comfort. It was not that there was nothing to love about winter, but the season turned so quickly from an astonishing orange and yellow autumn to a fog-land that was unsympathetic to those who had to slog back and forth in it. Snow, so eagerly anticipated as a childhood wonderland, was now only a wonder for two days at the most, for after that it became an obstacle in the daily course of school, work, buggies and babies.

The good things about winter were to be found in the food – ever-present reminders that somewhere and someday Earth would revert to its growing phase. Here, the natural world came alive in December and January because of the kitchen and dining table. It was in the moving to England, the living alongside other people in the cold, that some of us recognised the similarities in our home environments. Winter in England was when my mother first tasted mauby, the tree bark drink from the *Colubrina* species drunk all over the Caribbean, but not in Jamaica. In this island it is sorrel – the deep red drink made from a brew of island spices and sepals of the roselle plant, *Hibiscus sabdariffa* – that is the traditional Christmas-time drink. Sorrel and mauby, though they cannot grow in the British climate, helped my mother understand how we live with the natural world in different lands and come to similar conclusions. You will find the carmine-coloured sorrel flower all over the world, but until you interact – stop to smell and look and ask and try – you may pass a tasty opportunity by. The drink is such a well-known Jamaican December delicacy that it is sometimes called 'flower of Jamaica tea', or agua de

Jamaica in the Spanish-speaking Caribbean. Further afield, in West Africa where the plant is native, there are many other names to know: bissap in Senegal, where it is the national drink, wonjo in the Gambia, or zobo in Nigeria. Ask for karkadeh when speaking Arabic or request a sip of grajaeb juice in Thailand. 'Hibiscus tea' or 'roselle drink' might work in Europe but will receive puzzled looks in most of Jamaica, even though the very plant is in season from November through to the new year. You will find a variety of local expressions and uses for one thing.

During those winter gatherings, when family and friends were forced to meet indoors and spend more time in cosy settings away from the cold, they also traded traditions, picked up each other's style and recognised the similarities in each other's faces.

2000s
Grandfather

My grandfather approached the winter of his life and left England for the sunny side of the world. When he retired from working his job on the railways he left the London plane trees for the land of palm trees. It was a paradisiacal dream of his generation, to 'go home', but for many of them, home was where they had long got used to living in frosted times. Even my parents followed him and moved our young family to the island after many years in the cold.

I remember my grandfather as an old man with a gummy smile, a fresh brown suit and too much Brut. He would joke and dance and eat and seemed to enjoy life in those moments. It is only now I wish to ask about the days spent in the winter; was the same joy to be found?

Returned to the island of his birth, he realised that he was a product of time spent in a foreign land. I imagine he contemplated which land, which season was really the strange one. Where he once used to be able to put a gloved hand into a coat pocket in the middle of a storm and recognise a coin by the feel of its shape without looking at it, he now had to learn a new currency. He stared at the coins and notes for too long, trying to sort out the correct change and giving away his status as someone who was used to the olden days of shillings and ha'pennies.

He was used to midday tea and working in the rain because when rain is almost certain every day during a season, you had to splash on with it. When it rained in Jamaica, people dashed inside and tried to stay out of it as much as possible. You would venture out only for necessity – nothing of the tough waterproof boots and sturdy umbrellas and heavy coats to block the elements associated with wintry weather. If you *were* going to be in the rain here, he learned, better immerse yourself in it, even take off your shoes and accept being wet.

With the fog of old age settling in, setting and season seemed to soften into each other for my beloved. One day he would think he was in the parish of St Ann with my aunt and the next day his mind returned him to Kingston with me. At this winter of his being, the time and place shift held little importance to my grandfather: he was wherever he said he was and had endured enough of the shivers to be believed. By the time I was eleven, we obliged and dreamed ourselves into different people in different places to help him get through the spell. We knew not what the leap to the other side held for him, but we knew he had guided us through many earthly winters, and it was now our duty to help him through his personal one. His was a winter we could not see through; we gritted our teeth to bear it with sniffling noses and quivering lips. This same man had glimmered and greeted with a firm handshake, then a hug with hearty laughs. But after that growing season he seemed to shed like an autumn tree, waiting for the chill and still of the long, unavoidable sleep.

During the very last days of his seasons, my grandfather forgot me, a child who appeared in the mid-winter of his life when he had already started to retreat inside.

'Joan, come here darling, help me get up. I have to get to work.'

'Oh Pappy, yuh forgot me again? I'm not Auntie Joan, I'm Joan's niece, Petal's baby – your granddaughter – but I will help you. Where yuh going to today, Pappy, can I come?'

'Why yuh asking me silly questions, girl? Where else would I be going to work? British Rail, of course. Yuh can only come with me if you can haul and measure in winter storm. Anyways, make haste, I have to get out before the dark-sun to make it on time.'

'Sun already up, Pappy, sun always up here.'

'Be quiet and help me get up, Joan! You ever feel cold like this yet?'

'You alone cold, Pappy, the rest of us warm-warm. But can I still come with you? I never see winter or snow yet, plus I don't want you to go out there alone. I not afraid of it, Pappy, I want to come with you.'

'It is not your time, Joan, you will have your chance to follow me into the cold, let me clear the way first. For now, help me up before the day come to greet us.'

2020
Self

It has now been more than six years since I planted my own roots in the place my mother and grandfather lived; I now know my own British seasons as an adult and parent. Birds are less frequent and the rotting fruit that filled the air with its fermented punch a few months ago has disintegrated to naught. Even as I live this cycle each year, this unsettling season can burn holes of fatigue and fear where I want to bloom further than the boundaries of a bland vault of heaven. My elders did not have a name for this depression, yet it is impossible to ignore. There are days when the mood here seems to mimic the melancholy I associate with the fading memory of my mother and grandfather. I imagine it is what Nina

Simone felt when she sang for her elders in 'Another Spring'.

I understand the frustration with which my elders faced it, how it can hang over happy spirits. Even as one tries to stay bright enough to get on with a sunny spirit, the loss of life, of liveliness, can be such a shock to the body and mind that is in search of lustre and satisfaction. The life lived without winter takes place outdoors; it happens where people and things move and stop and move again, take stock, slowly interact, and then carry on again. There is no rushing inside to warm frozen fingers and the doors do not close quickly to keep in the heat. There are more chances to feel the pleasant wind, learn the names of colourful things and hear insects rattle in the night because these creatures are always there. There is the chance to stone a mango tree and then sit nonchalantly with the nectar running down your chin, in places that look like the abode of gods. We dance outside during every phase of Earth's cycle around the sun because we have been given this vivid thing, this place. The encounters with nature happen more often because of the setting, so there are some lessons that gather without effort. By six or seven, a sun isle child can go outside at daybreak and carefully snip peppermint or fever grass or lime leaf for their morning cup of tea. Maybe it is because the winter drives people indoors for months at a time, dries the land of green vine. Maybe it is easier to live this simply, this close to the source, in places where the season does not shift so drastically that everything withers and pretends to die.

In these moments, it is hard to remember spring on the other side. I like to walk the empty land and take new perspective on things that reveal entirely contrasting characteristics six months into the future. The seasonal slumber clears the way for dark thoughts to appear in the lonely corners of my mind; I do not wish to shy away from them for there is less to fear about the familiar.

Discarded snail shells crunch under unsuspecting feet and slug trails disappear when the creatures have nothing to eat. But bulbs burst through with green shoots, proving that the death and dread are only for a season. Perennial disappearance is not the winter's only feature, and those who pursue the colours of nature can find them if they have time to stop and seek. Snuff Mills, a park in northeast Bristol that runs alongside the River Frome, is like a runway of poised limbs, posed leggy, brown models. Snuff Mills, with its lime and horse chestnut trees that weep into the stream when leafy. Here, the river flows. It is no doubt icy, but it still flows and leads to somewhere else. Placing a twig or a piece of bark or a discarded shell in it might still pour the idea of you in some place faraway. Here, the trees light up with greens and yellows, lichens that take advantage of the climate where other organisms cannot. They spread their algal cells on the surface of trees that are themselves uninterested in blooming at that time of the year. The golden-orange colony on smooth barks of hawthorn and the grey-green crust on oak and ash do not mind what the rest of us avoid. They sometimes appear neon in contrast to the muted nature of everything else or like land-seaweed camouflaged in spiny branches of blackthorn bushes.

At the right time of the month, the moon sits in the sky, a perfect orb, shining over the resting city. This is the right time for a walk or bicycle ride around Bristol with that winter moon as the only guide. In full view of it, the icy midnight air that whips across your face does not seem so harsh when the want for it was your own desire. Evergreens create moonlit shadow shows, dancing and waving with the wind, while the bare branches of others enjoy the theatre of trees. Foxes creep around the city at this time and turn their heads in the middle of dimly lit roads to reveal the face that will reassure you that it is, indeed, not a cat. These graceful animals slide away with such ease that I think they must know precisely all the back paths and alleys into Bristol. The allure of winter is often found in the dark for me. Where girlfriends gather to begin the night, dress up and prance out in foxy get-ups of long coats and knee-high leather boots, through the parts of the city that do not sleep. The hot nights that start with standing frozen in nightclub lines are not nearly forgotten when that winter is recalled. The heaving séance of bodies swaying and sweating and shouting inside is deliverance, a place where you are encouraged to release the seasonal stress and warm worried bones – colder the day, better the night, joy wouldn't be so sweet if there was no plight.

At the start of the new day, I find myself seeking the shiny dark blue of the Eurasian magpie wing. This is one of the only birds that sticks around during every season here; it is unfair that the bird is vilified when they stay with us through dark times. Others flatter us with their presence when things are prosperous but they eventually flee when the habitat can no longer provide. Yet, hardy and without fear of a little cold, the magpies do not rely on the excesses of summer and spring. Every winter morning, they perch on tree beams and survey further, higher than we can see. Younger birds appear this time of year too, probably in their first winter on glossy new wings. Their dark feathers seem fluorescent – aquamarine, green and violet, contrasting the muffled features of their surroundings. I look for the metallic wings each day and hope to spot the crows before their rushed escape.

Magpies come raving with commanding chatter while robins bring delicate cheer to autumn mornings. One sweet robin builds a nest in my garden in the first year that a pandemic keeps us at home. It joins the late summer throng of little beaks nipping at birdfeeders; its shrill song is distinct even though it is outnumbered. It comes closer where others fly away, and it feels no need to hide its flaming underbelly from anyone's view. When the sparrows leave in the fall, the robin does not go along. Happier now to have its pick of seeds and louder without the competing voices. Children in countries with no winter see the bird in picture books about the season's thrill, yet the thing I want to learn most from the robin is self-confidence across settings.

In hope of brighter times, no sooner does the solstice hit its mark than we start to look out for signs of spring. No doubt, wintering is taxing. Even when claiming love for the cold here and speaking with dreamy eyes, that internal fire twinkles fiercer as the days inch longer and the snowdrops and daffodils open. These kinds of plants give us something beautiful to think about, a muse amidst the cracked black peppercorn tones of murky walks. For how can you stop and smell the roses where they are not in bloom, how does one hear birdsong that is not there? This burden of cold and colourlessness is never missed in lighter times and it is as if winter's bitter bite is struck from memory when the warmth returns; at least then your troubles are not the miseries of dark mornings and months. While faith is fickle to hold on to in unsure times, winter's fading is inevitable and the sun only hides. The animal chatter resumes and the tree shade welcomes us again, under whitebeam and maple, in soft grass with cherry blossom blanketing without snow. Winter's cyclical pursuit moves through the points where life and death are displayed, reflecting times long gone, and others yet to be made. Still, its ability to replenish and renew, to be entirely different in one place from the next, reflects a thing recreating itself. If we too spring and grow and then wither and die, can we not refresh and replenish too? In winter lies the assurance that, though the tether of our hearts is long and twisted, time is longer still.

Yielding

Amanda Thomson

I

Yield (n.) the influence of the sun on frost
The yield o' the day (phr.) the influence of the sun; also the height of the day

The morning after the clocks went back, it was 9:07 and the house was still in shadow. At 9:13, the sun tipped above the pinewood at the end of the field to the south and started to spill, weakly at first, into the living room, and it all felt better again. By mid-December the sun barely has the energy to rise above the trees at all, and as it makes its low curve westwards, the hills beyond that cast their long shadows down the strath. Any heat feels desultory at best, and the days often can't quite shake themselves free of the night before. Light can feel hard fought for, especially here, in the Highlands of Scotland, at 57° North, and everything feels more precarious.

On the winter solstice, a day lasts six hours forty minutes. 5pm can feel like midnight. Sunrise is at 8.53am and sunset 3:33pm, though if you are in the thickest part of the woods it can feel like dusk is at the back of two. In the long hours of darkness, when there's no moon, the stars pierce the sky in impossible numbers and brightness. Sometimes, on the cusp of autumn and winter, if the wind isn't rattling the trees too much or the rain isn't bouncing off the roof, we can step outside and hear the low bellow of stags rutting. On some days, the frost plays cat and mouse with the low path of the sun, trees casting white shadows for the whole length of the day; the frostline mimics the treeline, and whitened shadows on the grass shift and recede like the tide. The 'howe o' the year' is how the solstice is described in a nineteenth-century dictionary of the Scottish language. *Howe*: 'the middle, deepest or most intense part of a period of time, a season, etc., the dead; the declining portion (of day or year)'. Darkness pulls us close, invites us to slow down, reminds us of the limitations of our bodies.

II

Waller (n.) A confused crowd in a state of quick motion; as, *a waller of birds, a waller of bairns*, etc.
Flaught (n.) A considerable number of birds on wing; a flight; a flake of snow
Snell (adj.) Keen; severe; sharp; piercing (applied to the air)

In summer, when the sun is high, the spaces between the trees show light and bright green, dappled with shadow and with countless possibilities of ingress, but in winter, with low sun or low light, from a distance they seem impenetrable.

Still, once in the woods you stumble along paths hidden by the weight of summer growth. With the dieback of bracken and heather, rust-needle encrusted paths emerge and though we're not sure if they are human-formed or animal, they ask to be walked, just to see where they go. Sometimes they'll lead to a known path, or we'll walk them for a bit, then return the way we came if it feels as if we're going too far into the unknown. As that afternoon walk quickly becomes an evening stroll, there's that sudden fluttering in the stomach when you can't see as clearly as you should be able to. In the depths of winter, we deal in blacks and whites: in snow, pinewoods and birch stands become barcodes. And in the silence, this same snow gifts us tracks of animals and birds we wouldn't otherwise have known were here – hare, deer, badgers, and tinier imprints of mice and voles criss-cross and zigzag around the trees.

In winter, the Scots pines remain pine-green and the junipers sit low, their grey-green needles tightly held, as birds fly in for cover amongst their tangles. The larches, birches and rowans reveal their secrets and become entangled in a skyline clumsily cross-hatched with branches. Birds exist in silhouette, and even if there's no birdsong or their colours are darkened out in behind-light, we can still identify many. Long-tailed tits hang from the tips of twigs no thicker than their legs, and congregate with coal, great and blue tits, sometimes goldcrests and occasionally crested tits too. I pay chaffinches more attention than in summertime as they might be joined by wintering bramblings. So many birds gather in their winter flocks – sometimes in huge numbers – to better find food, for warmth, for protection.

One year a flock of three hundred redpolls spent two days restlessly scrabbling in the fields then flying back and forth between the junipers and the fringes of the Scots pines or amidst the birches and larches, and back down. Suddenly they rose as one from the ground and immediately scattered when a sparrowhawk came in low from the forest and split them. Flying in all directions, they disappeared.

On blue days when the air is snell, or in anticipation of it becoming so, ten, twenty coal tits, blue tits and great tits gather at the feeders, along with occasional woodpeckers, siskins and finches – gold, green, bull, chaff. When I go out to replace the fatballs, they fly behind, in front, overhead with a . . .

Thrrrrrrrrrrrrrrrrr

                                   Thrrrrrrrrrrrrrrrrrr

                 Thrrrrrrrrrrrrrr

                                   (say it)

so close and in stereo, ruffling the air like an express train speeding through a smaller Highland station on its way south to Glasgow or Edinburgh.

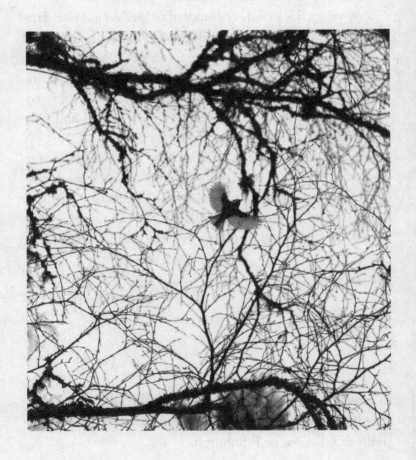

III

Louther (v.) to be entangled in snow or mire; to walk with difficulty
Creep (adv.) Cauld creep; that sensation of rigor which extends itself over the
surface of the body in consequence of exposure to severe cold, or of some
sudden alarm

While winter offers up different possibilities of walking, there are some walks that are year-round, and help us mark the change of seasons. Different flowers come and go – snowdrops, primroses, celandines are among the first to appear; scabious and harebells among the last – and spring-to-summer greens mellow to the greens, greys, umbers and maroons of autumn and winter.

From the house, beyond the trees, a ridge of hills stretches away in the distance. They're within walking distance, in theory, though we usually only make it to the lower slopes; beyond this the terrain is pathless and heather-thick and it would be a long trudge to reach the cairns at the top. Last winter, on a gunmetal grey day, the fields were white and it felt as if land and sky had been inverted. The birches lining the track were so laden with snow that their branches and the spindly tips of their trunks arched over our heads, and we ran from under them in case they gave way. In snowy silence we heard an occasional slither then the wet thud of snow dragged low from branches by its own weight, and once, a sharp crack and we knew somewhere within the pines there'd be the red raw splinter of a branch newly sheared under the leaden, white weight. For a little while we followed the tracks of a brown hare that had imprinted its pattern 1, 1, 2; 1, 1, 2; 1, 1, 2 until it veered off again beyond the birches, towards the older pines.

Looking south from the tops of these local-to-us hills are some of the highest mountains in Britain, the Cairngorms. It's there we'll see the earliest scoutherins of snow. These tops constitute a landmass that's described, variously, as high montane, arctic-alpine and the charity Plantlife tells me 'the most extensive areas of acidic arctic-boreal heaths in Britain', a massif that is the largest tract of high land in the UK (and I can't believe that there's a place so close to where I stay that can be described as 'arctic-alpine'!). They can be magical, other-worldly places with extreme conditions. There's an automatic weather station at the summit of Cairngorm run by Heriot-Watt University Physics Department and it has recorded top wind speeds of 176 mph. Windchill can drop the temperature to minus 20°C. Anything surviving up there must be exceptionally hardy.

In cracks and corries snow lies all year round, and partial melts feed lochs and lochans and river sources that I'll never get to. 'Snow-bed' communities of plants – liverworts, mosses and grasses with evocative names like snow fork-moss, scorched rustwort, monster paw-wort – grow on the plateau and I wonder if I've walked past, or on, any of these rare species without noticing. Residual snow lingers well into spring, sometimes to summer. The pinprick dots of whites we can see from these local peaks would be two, three, five metres across were we to reach them. There are snow patches that have only fully melted a handful of times in the last century, and some are assiduously monitored for the effects of climate change.

My partner and I love hillwalking but we're cautious with it, well aware of the limits of our navigation skills and our bodies, as well as the vagaries of Scottish weather. I've been hillwalking in Scotland since I was a teenager, but she grew up in a city on the other side of the world, where winter means bright blue skies and snow that lies for weeks and weeks, and there's a cold so keen it shocks, freezing nostril hair and eyelashes. How strange it was to spend a couple of winters there with her after a lifetime of Scottish winters, in a place where blue-sky-bright-snow banished the need for SAD lamps and vitamin D. Yet how we missed these hills.

For us, there's a point in the year when the tops of the Cairngorms, never mind their recesses, are out of bounds. We're no Nan Shepherds or Seton Gordons, and the places they describe, particularly in winter, are too high, too far away, a little bit too exposed and too far out of our comfort zones and skill sets. The tantalising glimpses of these mountains that we get from afar is enough.

IV

Eith-ken (adj.) Well known, easily recognisable. Usu. applied to animals which bear some distinguishing mark upon them either of colour or shape
Unco (n) 1. Anything strange or prodigious 2. A strange person: a stranger
Skugways (adv.) In a clandestine way, with a design to hide one's self

There are creatures in these uppermost reaches of Scotland's landmass, and although you can go for a whole day's walking without seeing much more than a pipit, you're always looking out for eagles, or a peregrine. Dotterel arrive in spring and leave at the end of the summer, but all year round you'll find snow buntings, ptarmigan and mountain hares, though they rarely reveal themselves.

Rock Ptarmigan are only found in the highest parts of Scotland. Specialists of tundra and sub-arctic/alpine vegetation and habitats, they have the capacity to survive the most extreme conditions. They moult three times a year with the seasons to adapt to the habitat, to better evade detection by predators that rely on sight. The Scottish Ornithologists' Club's *The Birds of Scotland* tells me that ptarmigan are mottled brown in summer and turn white in winter, with a grey phase which Scottish birds keep for longer than other subspecies. They hold onto some grey feathers throughout, a 'cryptic colouration' that's probably adapted because of the unpredictable weather that leads to more erratic snow cover. Their propensity to be near rocks means they can hide from both visual predators and shelter from the weather and they'll dig snow holes, too, if cold or a storm calls for it.

On these upper slopes bound mountain hares, who also change their coats to suit the season, a camouflage designed to protect themselves from those eagles I'm endlessly hoping for as I walk, and foxes too. The Scottish mountain hare also moults three times a year, sometimes retaining its brown summer coat with its bluish grey underfur into early winter when it will turn white. When moulting, in its in-between stages, its coat will have patches of brown and white.

One bitterly cold day, as we walked the lower slopes of a mountain with no intention of getting to its top, flurries of snow whipped around us as a hare louped up across a snow-field, and then vanished when it stopped and couried down. I looked away and then back and I knew it was still there, but couldn't get my binoculars on it again. I scanned the snowfield and wasn't sure whether what I was looking at was a tussock of heather poking through the snow or the hare's lugs. Then it was up and off, over the ridge with a speed that belied the depth of snow it bounded across.

There's a vastness to this landscape, and even if there's a steady stream of walkers you'll see sometimes just the tini-est of specks on a horizon line, and you'll have to look twice to see if they are people, deer or rocks. You'll see bright dots of red, blue, mustard, purple Gore-Tex a couple of miles further on or behind, and congregations form at cairns, or where people stop to catch their breaths or tracks converge. Dotterel, buntings, ptarmigan and mountain hares are so infrequently seen. It's usually a movement out of the corner of your eye that alerts you, and even then, once they're at rest you have to really peer to find them. Sometimes you have to stop and scan the landscape, crouched down below any horizon-line so that you too become, for a time, a part of the land. Dotterel can sit so still, their mottled plumage exactly matching the grassy tussocks and shadows and light of the high moor; ptarmigan blend with the granite and grasses and the last, dirty patches of snow, and it's so easy to miss them if they stand stock-still; the mountain hare is just another mound of snow until it bounds away.

When I do see a ptarmigan or a mountain hare, it always feels like a gift. They are, of course, striking creatures. But I love how they hide in plain sight, and that it's these kind of places where they are to be found.

V

To dare (v) to be afraid, to stand in awe

Growing up in Scotland, it's been easy to feel both visible and invisible, sometimes at the same time – here, like everywhere else, race, ethnicity, gender, sexuality can all come into play – but I've never felt estranged from the country, the countryside, or from getting out into nature. Quite the opposite in fact: I feel much more at home living in the rural north of Scotland than I ever felt in all my years of Central Belt city living. Any hesitancy in getting out into nature has related to longer routes and remoteness and is entirely sensible: these places can be scary and dangerous, and I try not to treat being in them blithely. Vulnerability is a strange thing. There have been times, even when I've known exactly where I am out in the hills, when I've still felt exposed and just too far away. And then there have been times that I've been out in Glasgow, London, Chicago, walking home, wherever that may have been – sometimes at night, sometimes during the day – when I've felt an instinctive, proprioceptive bodily fluttering too, and that's a different kind of vulnerability altogether.

Recently, in early winter, on a rare, calm day with a sky-blue sky and sub-zero temperatures and when the Mountain Weather Information Service assured us that winds would be minimal and the chances of cloud-free tops would be 90%, we did go up onto the plateau. As it turned to late morning we walked up Miadan Creag an Leth-choin – the Lurcher's Crag – on these first skirvins of snow, and the sun still hadn't crested above the tops. We walked in shadow towards a thin, bright halo of cloud that softened and brightened the horizon lines, smooth, then jagged at the Northern Corries. Ice had thickened the blades of grass and we skited on the occasional rock coated with the thinnest of icy layers. We wondered if we should have brought walking poles or crampons, but in the end, it was okay. Over to the west, clouds conflated land and sky, and we knew anyone at the top of these far peaks would be seeing just a sea of grey below, with Cairn Gorm, Ben Macdui and the plateau between them distant islands above. As the day went on, the sun sat low without ever, really, having climbed, and had no influence on the ground beneath our feet. The cold pierced our down jackets and pinched our noses. Even though we knew exactly where we were, even with all the other walkers making the most of this rare day, we felt, keenly, our smallness and fragility. Still, any vulnerability up here would be of our own making.

As we walked at a thousand metres up, the ground before us was crisp and glistening. We spotted a set of tracks, a ptarmigan's footprints – 1, 2, 3, 4, 5, then the slightest brush of feather against the snow, and nothing more. We stopped, raised our binoculars and scanned the hillside to see if the bird was still present, but we just couldn't locate it, and wondered if it was hiding or watching us in plain sight.

The definitions at the top of each section are from: J. Jamieson's *Dictionary of the Scottish Language* (Edinburgh: William P Nimmo, 1867); and Dictionaries of the Scots Language, https://dsl.ac.uk. All photographs in this piece by Amanda Thomson.

Mud

Alys Fowler

It was hard, rutted and ruined in places with craters that dulled to grey dust on their edges, but, as paths go, it was pretty steadfast. Then the autumn rains came and softened all those ruins, dampened the grey back to brown and then black and it became something moveable. People started to step around the soft bits that were beginning to squelch and suck at loose boots and shoes as if it might be in the business of stealing them. Now, in the depth of winter, those soft bits are puddled with pools of water and the path has taken on new directions as people try and tiptoe around all this mud.

I read these paths as I walk them daily. I can't help it. It's a lifelong habit of looking at my feet for small details. I smell these paths as I walk them; the sweet rot of autumn is now giving way to something a little more metallic with a hint of sulphur in the worst spots. I feel these paths as I walk them, physically as I slurp and slip, but on some emotional level too. They are wounded to me, hardening in the summer from the previous winter's damage, like scar tissue, reopening in the winter, rotting and foetid.

Is it too dramatic to feel this way about paths? They are merely desire lines that snake in and out and around the park I live next door to in Birmingham. They are not official; they speak of quick routes to hidden spots, of how to journey unseen, or out of the rain, to places where you can sit on fallen trees or build dens. They travel through the little woodland, up and out around the edge of the marshy spot, back into the thicket that edges the pond that is slowly silting up, past the great twisted copper beech, which has contorted one turn too many and been condemned by the tree surgeon; it stands limbless, awaiting its fate when it will rot slowly away. Up past the Scots pine where the parakeets holler at bedtime, just as the late evening sun turns its whole trunk a golden apricot and past the holly with its lone ghost-white branch, where the genetics have regressed all use of photosynthesis like the first streak of grey hair at the temple of the head. Here, you have a choice: you can turn right up to the gate or go on deep into the cherry laurels with their masses of dead wood that give rise to wood ear fungus the size of my palm. Fungus which, if you can get the weak winter sun to catch it, looks almost pink and human, as if the trees have sprouted ears to eavesdrop on the happenings beneath their thick canopy of rainproof leaves. Last year it was a nest for young lovers, this year it is home to the frantic slap, slap, slap and acrid smell of heroin cooking and the dull bickering until the hit takes hold. But I took the turning right and have gone through the gate.

On the other side of the park, where the springs rise, the situation with the paths is far worse. I go every so often to visit the large stand of beech trees and look at my world from a different perspective and here the paths are a quagmire by late winter, too wet for anything other than wellington boots. Their clag seeps down through the many rivulets from the springs that appear in the wet months and slicks over the one circular concrete path in the park, so that this too is a muddy experience. But this side of the park is not my concern, so I merely go to peer at its soft or frozen or hardened mass, as a reminder of why I work.

All winter long, when no one is looking, in the bleak mornings or the lost hours after lunch, before the gloaming hits, I go to work to repair the paths. I have been doing this for years because it is how I get back and forth to the allotment and thus it is my daily tread, my path to happiness.

Mud isn't a state of winter soils, it's a product of too much pounding – whether by rain or feet – and of too little organic matter. Mud is soil mixed with water; specifically, it is the clay or silt particles made loose in water. Whereas soil wants to be firmly rooted, mud wants to go places, it oozes out of its home. It sticks, coats and clings to all that it touches. It wants to move on.

Mud moves because its particles are no longer knitted together by gossamer-thin threads of fungi and the microbiology of billions of small lives that make up the structure of the soil. Clay is soluble, and with the addition of water, this intricate world dissolves. Water's pull on clay is so strong that it dictates a whole new order.

When a single clay particle meets a single water one, it becomes married to it through a negative ionic charge. Put a whole bunch of these couplings together and they all get in formation, add pressure and the clay begins to yield into shape. It starts to have plasticity. It becomes active. Too much water and it will be a soup, too little and it will lose its elasticity, but just in the middle is the dream spot, beloved of potters; less so for canal builders, who were said to have to carry a 'Man-tool', a little hand-carved wooden spade the size of your palm, necessary to remove the clay from boots and tools, which would weigh the worker down. The tool was in itself 'like another man' in how much it lightened the load.

The more clay particles in the mud, the more plasticity it has so that it can whip into waves with fissures or craters and indentations of all those who went before. Silt makes a loose, thin mud that can't hold onto the water for long, but clay is a different matter. It has a memory. It will remember the shape it has previously been in; work it hard enough and it won't ever forget it. Potters know all about this memory; get it right and the pot yields to form, get it wrong and the cracks appear.

The more plastic the clay becomes, the more memory it has. The same negative ionic charges that bond the clay to water, also orient the clay particles so that they stack. If you were to roll a slab of clay, like a piece of pastry, and then bend one corner up before rolling it flat again and then firing it, the whole piece would be flat and hard apart from that one corner, which would have a slight bend in it. Even though it had been rolled flat, even though it had been fired. That corner, those clay particles, would remember that they had once been bent. Clay remembers its past and wants to return to it again and again and again. Add water to my paths and the clay in the soil recalls every foot, every slam, every step.

If you can't exactly make the clay forget, you can send it back to the beginning. Keep adding water to the clay and, because the particles are soluble, the balance of plasticity will be lost and the substance will turn into a suspension. This is the puddle on the path or soupy slip the potter uses to keep the clay moist on a wheel.

Which is one of the reasons why the worst bits of my paths, the muddiest slicks, return at the first sign of heavy rain. The heavy clay that makes up my Midland soil is ready to jump back into formation of all the many boots and trainers, of tricycle wheels and paw prints, that have thumped it into puddles.

Mud has a memory and it also has a history, one as old as time. It is in the first chapter of the origin story; it lines the pond that holds the primordial soup that life crawls out of. But in these early days it never knew how to stay still. When the world was still young, storms would rage, weathering rocks and stripping continents and coastal areas as rivers of silt and clay would run into the seas, leaving behind a land of barren rock. Along ancient shorelines of Bolivia, you can find heaps of the earliest fossilised fish that died 460 million years ago, choked to death on flash flooding that washed mud down from rivers and flooded the coast. Thick masses of smothered fish appear in the rocks of a similar age around the world. Life would get going and then ... bam! Mud would swallow it up.

But then something radical begins to happen to mud. It starts to flourish. It begins with fungi and then really takes hold with land plants as their network of roots give mud something to stick to. Between 458 and 359 million years ago the amount of mud on the earth increases tenfold. The first deep-rooted plants, early primitive trees and cycads start to knit together the surface of the earth. Sediment that has previously been whipping around the earth in rageful storms suddenly slows as the mud clings to the roots of plants and becomes soil full of life.

Rivers start to form banks and wetlands appear; this shifts the way the water flows and life on earth as we know it starts to take hold. There are a few other players in the dramatic increase in mud: together with plant roots, many different fungi, bacteria, protea and other soil microbes all come together to start to accelerate the breakdown of rocks into fine particles; they build soils and this slows run-off further. This then allows thick layers of mud to pile up in river valleys and create alluvial plains, which in turn create wetlands and marshes rich in life, forming some of the most significant hunting and gathering grounds for early humans.

At every stage of mud's early history, it aids life – even when it is smothering fish, it's creating rich layers of sediment. Mudrock – that is the layers of mud that have been pressed down by time into something hard – is the most abundant rock in geological record and accounts for roughly half of all sedimentary formations. So much of our world comes from that mudrock.

When weathered and broken down, it gives back the clay particles to make mud again. But this time it is Clay++. Clay is the most reactive particle in any soil; it is charged and like a magnet it attracts good things to it. Between the layers of ancient, hardened mud are banks of minerals, nutrients and organic matter. Mudrock, for instance, is a rich source of potassium, a nutrient essential to all plant growth.

Mud builds life. It made our first pots, which allowed us to start cooking instead of just roasting. It created the means to mark our earliest writing, the cuneiform clay tablets of Mesopotamia. It helped create our first buildings with wattle and daub and then eventually bricks. It makes our plates and cups, it tiles our bathrooms and fills our cat's litter tray. It colours our world with pigments, it even coats this page you're reading. Kaolin, a soft white clay, is used in papermaking – it gives the shine to every glossy magazine and to every crumpled advert shoved through your letter box.

Geologists like to say that mud is both a beginning and an end; the other way that mud plays a significant part in our world is that it fuels it. If you go deep down into the mudstone you'll find layers of organic matter, pressed and hardened into coal, petroleum, gas and oil. Ancient mud is everywhere; it is natural and necessary to all life on earth.

But around 20,000 years ago, the picture changes; it shifts slowly at first and then it starts to speed up until around 5,000 years ago. At this point it alters so drastically that mud no longer has a natural history. The cause of that shift is us. 20,000 years ago, we started to tend to plants and animals, to select and nurture them; 10,000 years ago we began to seriously domesticate them and 5,000 years ago we got so good at it that we expanded our people and our places. We became farmers that produced animals, cereals, fruits, vegetables, and with them, mud.

Of course, we weren't actively farming mud, but as we started to cut down forests to make way for plant crops and animals, we increased soil erosion. The rates of this shot up, and even more sediment began to fill the rivers and valleys and they flooded and changed course. Once these shifting landscapes settled, they gave rise to more tidal flats and alluvial plains with rich fertile soils, and so we started to get really good at farming. Again, we expanded our people, our places. And we've kept on doing that, producing food, making people, creating mud.

Our mud production got so good that you could start to stratify the different layers that built up through the Anthropocene. There is 500-year-old colonial-era sediment in southern America that leads you to believe that all streams have deep, high banks, until the mud is dragged away to reveal the rich, black soil of pre-European arrival. There is early industrial mud of mines and factory waste that was often released directly into waterways or spread as slurry across fields. Or late industrial muds, such as red mud, a highly alkaline waste product of the aluminium industry, or the muds left behind from copper and gold mining. These are held in huge mud dams and the world confronts a swelling problem of muddy mine tailings that are increasingly bursting their holdings. These toxic muds spew over towns and villages, killing thousands and polluting the land that they seep across.

Maybe it is better not to call it Anthropocene mud, because it isn't being made by all humans, just some. It is a product of capitalism, all this mud that is sloshing and oozing and squishing and sticking and spreading about. If ancient mudstone builds life, Capitalocene mud, which is only just beginning to be packed down and hardened into sedimentation, does quite the opposite. It smothers and ruins.

Which brings me back to my path, which is very much human-made, if on a smaller scale. Every winter brings rain that turns it from something solid to something I have to slurp and slide along. With it, my old dog becomes more and more reluctant to come out. She picks out each muddy paw with such delicate disdain as she attempts and often fails to try and make her way along the thin, bramble-edged bank of the path before skidding back into its pools.

It is not odd for an oft-trodden path to get muddy in winter, but it is getting worse each year. The path has too many users. You can't blame anyone for this, or put another way, I certainly don't want to be the one who is accused of using it too much. There is an argument for encouraging a more diffuse use of the space; if everyone just picked their own way through the space rather than funnelled through in a single thread, then it might fare better. But then that's the point of a path: it is a desire line to a destination and, as the dog would testify, walking through brambles is not fun.

When I first started walking this path, my allotment was covered with brambles and dock; it was thick with couch grass and had a huge dead conifer, which someone had rightly decided to chop down but didn't know what to do with. It lay ghostly over the back of the plot and needed to be clambered over. There were no paths to the shed and there wasn't a compost heap to be seen. It took several years of dedicated winter work to order it back into something resembling a plot. I built a brick path, scouring skips for suitable frost-proof sorts; I built a fruit cage and a poly-tunnel, compost bins, a tiny pond and buried the conifer into a Hugelkultur bed so that it could slowly rot down, feeding the plants for the next twenty years.

Daily, I would walk the park path, learning its twists and turns by heart, watching it change subtly over the seasons and years. One year a hawthorn fell right across the path and for a good long while I clambered over, whilst the dog ran under its trunk. Then it sank into the earth and I could step over and the dog had to leap. Meanwhile, others started to meander round it and thus the path did too and it seemed silly to keep to the old route, so the dog and I joined in.

Eventually, when I had pulled at every dock and smoth-ered the best of the couch grass and poured love in the form of compost, manure and leaf mould into the beds so that they had risen to the soft soil that I think of as mine, I had little to do on the allotment in the winter. The allotment could be tucked up under a layer of mulch and my work was done till spring. I still go daily – it's a ritual, to say hello and poke about a bit. But I am always itching for purpose in these darker months, so a few years ago, I turned a different sort of attention to the paths. I decided, unasked and unappointed, to become the paths' custodian and to try and sort them out.

When I first started walking this path, I was married to a man. I lived a different life on the same path, but once I had learnt the twist and turns of my own heart, watching it change, I realised that, much like the path, I didn't have to keep to the same route. I came out. The two halves of my life, straight and bent, walk this path; perhaps this is also why I try to fix them. I am maintaining the thread back to my ghost self, whilst forging a road ahead for my future one.

As I put this down here on the page, I realise how odd it sounds, a middle-aged woman fixing paths in the park in secret. But I am born for this task. I get to play in the mud like a child and become utterly absorbed in my journey. And the bit I like best is that it is anonymous. If it works, no one even knows I've done it. When I get it right, I can point to a whole stretch where the path looks, well, just like a path: dark, strong, singular and stable. So perfect that you don't even take notice of it; instead, you are assessing how you'll take on the muddy bit ahead. Hidden in the middle is my secret and every time I step down on the good bits of the path, a little shiver of delight runs up through my body.

The bits I don't get right are another thing, a source of daily irritation as I unpick them and try again.

The path is failing, of course, because of the mud, which is appearing because of pounding and the rain, which is increasing the negative ionic bonds between the clay that is reorientating its particles, stealing the space for air. This in turn is making the soil anaerobic; it is causing metallic and sulphurous smells as the oxygen-loving bacteria is replaced by the sulphurous kind that can withstand the foetid conditions. As this happens all sort of other oxygen-loving microbes and fungi start to fail and as they give up their work, so does the structure of the soil.

As the space for air and gas exchange gets less, water can no longer filter in and out; it gets trapped and the soil's resistance to erosion dissipates. All the binding agents – plant roots and fungal hyphae, organic matter and microscopic critters – start to decompose and if at this moment a disturbance happens – a runner or many runners hammering the earth – the stuff that all this life is holding together starts to break down. And with it goes the structure that can hold the footfall of all those pounding feet or that intrepid eleven-year-old who's desperate for a mountain to bike or the lost parent who thought it might be suitable for a pram, or me and my dog.

This process of losing soil structure can be rapid or slow; it is not unnatural but can be sped up or slowed down by good soil management. A centimetre of good soil, that is, one with good structure and fertility, takes about 500 years to make. I'm with the American author, essayist and environmentalist Edward Abbey who, when asked what he stood for in life, said,

'I stand for what I stand on.' I guess I've made it my mission in life to make sure that the soil I stand upon is not unnecessarily lost. On a practical level, I fix the path because I need to go somewhere, but on a spiritual level I fix it because I want future critters of all kinds to get places too.

My path runs through a very small wood. It's merely a thicket; my 'countryside self' laughs at this city adult who thinks forty trees make a wood. But it is the closest I get to one, so that is what I call it. The wood is made up of an ancient hedgerow with mighty 400-year-old oaks that once marked the boundaries of a field system. The park was originally a farm and if you look across the parkland you can trace the peaks and dips of the drainage system: the ridges and furrows from the medieval open field system. Down one side runs the old hedge and built up on its other side are little thickets of woodland, mostly of 40- to 60-year-old oak, ash, holly and poplar, a few graceful beech trees and a lot of hazel planted as the result of some scheme, no doubt. When I first came to the park this hazel had had little or no management and before my path-building days, I secretly coppiced it. I grew up amongst coppiced woodlands in Hampshire and although I had absolutely no right to go about coppicing my urban parkland, I also figured I had no right not to, particularly when, one early spring, I found wood anemones growing and my desire to restore their habitat overtook worrying about permission.

I started to coppice and for a while another bloke did the same. I'm not sure if he had permission either, but we'd cross paths and before you knew it there was quite a lot of coppiced wood to be had. And, perhaps not by chance, this coincided with the rise in mud; the woodlands were now more appealing to walk through, no longer dense and dark, and this led to the decline in the path. One thing leads to another.

There are many ways to fix a path that is too wet. One way is to build away from the problem, but this requires tools, perhaps machinery and certainly permission. I had none of these, so I used what was to hand: the wood around me.

This is how I fix my paths: I take the thin poles of the coppiced hazel and with these any other suitable fallen branches and I lay them down into the soft mud, side by side, like lines on a page. It's an old technique known as a corduroy path or road. Logs or poles are placed perpendicular to the direction of the path or road over low, swampy or muddy places, so there is something for the foot, hoof or tire to hold onto. If done right, the poles laid out together look like corduroy fabric.

It's an ancient solution, one up, perhaps, from stepping stones. You can find versions made by the Roman Empire, like the one in the Archaeological Museum in Hamburg, which houses part of the Wittmoor bog track, used to travel across an otherwise inaccessible bog. We even have our own, much older version in the UK; it's slightly different in design, but it follows the same principles. It's known as the Post Track and was built by Neolithic farmers on the Somerset Levels. An ancient causeway that dates from around 383 BCE, it was made from lime and hazel posts laid on the ground with long planks of ash and oak laid on top. Apparently, the track was maintained, replaced and updated over many generations, until it eventually succumbed to the elements. It was said that it led to places of spiritual significance.

I get that. Like the Neolithic farmers, I too am building my own path to places of significance to me. Perhaps, then, my secretive path-building is less odd than I think; perhaps wayfinding is written in my DNA.

I love this hunt for suitable branches and leftover coppiced hazel, placing one after another, selecting and sizing so that it all fits together. I can spend hours doing it. I scan the ground, backtracking on myself when I find the perfect thickness of wood further on. It drives the dog nuts at the beginning of the season, but by deep winter she is more resigned and takes herself off snuffling.

When I get it right, it stays in place; when I get it wrong, runners, furious with what they must see as trip hazards, uproot my design and on more than one occasion, I've seen some daft dog run off with a stick so wide it can't get it out of the woods. I used to smart if the poles and branches were upturned from the path. I wondered if I should leave posters explaining the method. I felt annoyed that others couldn't see the obvious work, but I've learnt that the discarded poles are my master. I have chosen the wrong pieces and need to start again.

Sometimes I run thin on good material; coppicing doesn't happen every year and in the years between, I scavenge through the brambles for fallen dead wood and logs.

The right kind of punk wood is brilliant stuff, soft and squidgy, only a short time away from being broken down. It is almost compost.

Pressed down into the mud, this light dead wood acts as a sponge, absorbing the water around it. It doesn't take long in the right depth of mud for it to disappear as it sinks into its burial spot. The coppiced hazel settles into the soil much more slowly. The satisfaction of these coppiced poles is that if you can get the timing right and you have a mud soft enough, but not too watery, it will stick to the poles, it will form around and hold them in place, so that all winter long there's something to land on, but with every foot pounding it down, the poles slowly sink under so that by spring you can barely see they are there. When this happens, when the poles sink back to where they came from, this is when the real path-building begins.

In both cases, the wood is acting as a platform to redistribute weight over the soil, but once buried into the mud, a whole other world takes over. Here the microbial critters and diminutive life, the arbuscular mycorrhizal fungi and the bacteria that had given up in the anaerobic conditions, go back to work breaking down this new source of organic matter and breathing life back into the soil.

The soil is made up of the living, the recently dead and the long gone. The recently dead create the organic matter in the soil. This is made up of all the many dead things you can find there: the bodies of plants, animals and fungi as well as all the corpses of microbes and the substances that these microbes synthesise. A seemingly endless procession of big things that ate little things that ate smaller things that ate tiny things that ate the things smaller than that, rotting back into the earth. If you were to peer at it very closely down a microscope, you could still discern where it has come from, you could see the dead bit of wood or animal bone or microbe bodies. Soil organic matter is by no means at the end of rotting; it is on its way to becoming something else.

It still has many more rounds in the tumble dryer of the soil food web as it is redigested by things like earthworms and other fungi and recycled again and again by different microbes and bacteria. When it has been further weathered and chemically processed and you can no longer tell which bit was once what, then it becomes humus.

Humus is magic. It has gone the full cycle of being dead; it is very dead and that makes it a very stable substance. All the other organic material is in flux, but humus has come to a standstill. It is also, weirdly, jelly-like, so it's a wobbly sort of standstill. It can last anywhere from ten to 1,000 years. It sticks around in more ways than one: it's actually glue-like and it binds to other particles in the soil; its stability makes the soil more so. It can hold up to ten times its own weight in water and it is highly charged.

And here's the bit that makes my heart race, that thrills me to think of when I land on the bits of the path that were once mud but are now stable: humus loves clay, in fact, it's got more sway over clay than water. Both clay and humus are colloidal; clay is flaky in appearance and humus is jelly-like and together they suck up to each other and bond fast. If you want humus to stick around in your soil, if you want it to be there in a 1,000 years' time, you give it a partner of clay because it protects the humus from being further broken down by biological decomposition, as all those microbes can't go to work. The clay wraps the humus in a protective coat and allows it to linger on into the future.

Together the humus and the clay become a powerhouse of good soil. The soil becomes more stable through good structure; the clay is bonded to the humus, instead of the water, which means it no longer wants to move about, it doesn't want to be soup. This means the soil has more porosity; there are spaces between the particles and this allows the water and oxygen to move through the soil better, which in turns allows life in the soil to thrive. The more diversity of life in the soil, the better the structure. All those fine threads of life make for a soil that many feet can pound along, that many paws can patter on.

And the most stable humus in the soil, that 1000-year-old stuff, nearly always started off life as wood. The hardest parts of wood are cellulose and lignin – they take the longest to break down – but they do and when they get almost to the very end and meet a clay particle, they make very stable humus, something that is thought of as the lifeforce of good soil.

Those hazel poles and fallen branches will one day become humus. They are going that way regardless of me and whether I press them into the soil or not, everything rots back eventually. But in the meantime, I get to tread my path a little more sure-footedly, deep in the knowledge that, one day, when no one remembers me or my words, the soil below will be building future ways forward.

From *Sir Gawain* and the Green Knight

So the festival finishes and a new year follows
in eternal sequence, season by season.
After lavish Christmas come the lean days of Lent
when the flesh is tested with fish and simple food.
Then the world's weather wages war on winter:
cold shrinks earthwards and the clouds climb;
sun-warmed, shimmering rain comes showering
onto meadows and fields where flowers unfurl;
woods and grounds wear a wardrobe of green;
birds burble with life and build busily
as summer spreads, settling on slopes as
              it should.
      Now every hedgerow brims
      with blossom and with bud,
      and lively songbirds sing
      from lovely, leafy woods.

So summer comes in season with its subtle airs,
when the west wind sighs among shoots and seeds,

and those plants which flower and flourish are a pleasure
as their leaves let drip their drink of dew
and they sparkle and glitter when glanced by sunlight.
Then autumn arrives to harden the harvest
and with it comes a warning to ripen before winter.
The drying airs arrive, driving up dust
from the face of the earth to the heights of heaven,
and wild sky wrestles the sun with its winds,
and the leaves of the lime lay littered on the ground,
and grass that was green turns withered and gray.
Then all which has risen over-ripens and rots
and yesterday on yesterday the year dies away,
and winter returns, as is the way of the world
          through time.

– Simon Armitage

Notes on Contributors

Photo © Peter James Millson

SIMON ARMITAGE is the UK Poet Laureate. He was made CBE for services to poetry in 2015, and in 2019 received the Queen's Gold Medal for Poetry. He was Oxford Professor of Poetry from 2015 to 2019. He has published twelve full-length collections, most recently *Magnetic Field* (Faber, 2020). He is a broadcaster, playwright, novelist, and the author of three best-selling volumes of non-fiction. His play *The Last Days of Troy* was performed at Shakespeare's Globe Theatre. Over the past three decades he has received numerous accolades including the 2017 PEN Award for Poetry in Translation and an Ivor Novello Award for his lyrics in the BAFTA-winning television film 'Feltham Sings'. A translator of medieval poetry, his version of *Sir Gawain and the Green Knight* has sold over 150,000 copies worldwide. He lives in Yorkshire and is Professor of Poetry at the University of Leeds.

Photo © Tjaša Kalamar

KALIANE BRADLEY is an Anglo-Cambodian writer, editor and critic based in London. Her fiction and narrative non-fiction has appeared in *The Offing*, *Catapult*, *Granta*, *The Tangerine* and *The Willowherb Review*, among other publications. Her dance and theatre criticism has appeared in *Exeunt*, *The Stage*, *Time Out*, *Springback Magazine* and the *Observer*. She is currently Associate Editor at *Springback Magazine* and a commissioning editor at Penguin Press. She has previously been a commissioning editor for Granta Books and an editorial director at 3 of Cups Press. In 2021 she received an Arts Council England grant to write her debut novel, *The Lotus Demon*.

Photo © Carlo Pizzati

TISHANI DOSHI is a Welsh–Gujarati poet, novelist and dancer. Her most recent books are *Girls Are Coming Out of the Woods*, short-listed for the Ted Hughes Poetry Award, and a novel, *Small Days and Nights*, shortlisted for the RSL Ondaatje Prize and a New York Times Bestsellers Editor's Choice. *A God at the Door* (Bloodaxe Books), her fourth collection of poems, was published in spring 2021. She lives in Tamil Nadu, India. www.tishanidoshi.com

Photo © Jennie Scott

BERNARDINE EVARISTO won the Booker Prize 2019 with her novel *Girl, Woman, Other*, the first black woman and black British person to win it. Her other novels are *Mr Loverman*, *Blonde Roots*, *Soul Tourists*, *Lara*, *The Emperor's Babe* and *Hello Mum* and her writing spans non-fiction, literary criticism, drama and short fiction. Her many awards and honours include Author of the Year at the British Book Awards and an OBE, both in 2020. She is Professor of Creative Writing at Brunel University London, Honorary Fellow of St Anne's College, Oxford University, Vice President of the Royal Society of Literature, and President of Rose Bruford College of Theatre and Performance.
www.bevaristo.com

Photo © Ming de Nasty

ALYS FOWLER is a gardener by training and writes about the natural world around her. As she lives in a city, she takes her nature wherever she can get it: canals, railway lines, parks, waysides and scrubland. Her writing combines horticulture, biology and biography and in her acclaimed book *Hidden Nature*, she traces both the Birmingham canals and her coming out as a gay woman. Due to her training in horticulture she is particularly interested in the soil and all that lies in its hidden depths. She likes reading soil like you would a book and is often found digging down into things. She is also very good at making compost. She lives with her wife and small dog in Birmingham.

Photo © Anthea
Gellatly Photography

RAINE GEOGHEGAN is a poet, prose writer and playwright of Romany, Welsh and Irish descent. Nominated for the Forward Prize, Best of the Net and the Pushcart Prize, her work has been published online and in print with *Poetry Ireland Review*, *Travellers' Times*, *Ofi Press*, *Under the Radar*, *Fly on the Wall*, *Poethead* and many more. Her pamphlets *Apple Water: Povel Panni* and *They Lit Fires: Lenti Hatch O Yog* were published with Hedgehog Poetry Press and her work was featured in the film *Stories from the Hop Yard*, made by Catcher Media. Her first collection, *The Talking Stick: O Pookering Kosh* will be published with Salmon Poetry Press in March 2022.
www.rainegeoghegan.co.uk

Photo © Ruth Lawrence

JAY GRIFFITHS is the author of *Why Rebel; Pip Pip: A Sideways Look at Time*, which won the Discover Award for the best new non-fiction writer to be published in the USA; and *Wild*, which won the inaugural Orion Book Award and was shortlisted for both the Orwell Prize and a World Book Day Award. Other titles include *Kith: The Riddle of the Childscape*, *Tristimania*, *Anarchipelago* and *A Love Letter from a Stray Moon* (with a foreword by John Berger). She has broadcast for the BBC and was a recent Hay Festival International Fellow. She has written for Radiohead's newspaper, for the Royal Shakespeare Company, and for various publications including the *Guardian*.
www.jaygriffiths.com

Photo © Mary McCartney

JACKIE KAY is a Scottish poet, novelist and nonfiction writer. She is the author of a number of works, including *The Adoption Papers, Trumpet* and *Red Dust Road*. Between 2016 and 2021, she served as Scotland's Makar or national poet. The recipient of numerous prizes, she was also twice shortlisted for the Scottish Book of the Year Award. She is currently chancellor of the University of Salford, and divides her time between Glasgow and Manchester. She was made a CBE in 2019.

Photo © Nicholas Axelrod

MICHAEL MALAY is a writer and teacher based in Bristol. He spent his early years in Jakarta, Indonesia, before moving to Australia with his family at the age of ten. He is the author of *The Figure of the Animal in Modern and Contemporary Poetry* and is currently working on a book called *Late Light*, a book about eels, mussels, crickets and moths. His writing has been published in *The Willowherb Review*, *Wasafiri* magazine and *Dark Mountain*, and he plays central midfield for the Easton Cowfolk, an anti-racist football club that has links with teams all around the world, including Palestine, Mexico, Italy, and Germany.

Photo © Katie Marland

PIPPA MARLAND is an author and academic, based at the University of Bristol. Her research, currently funded by the Leverhulme Trust, focuses on nature writing, especially the representation of small islands and farming communities. Her creative writing draws on her childhood experiences of living in Ghana, Malta, west Wales, and the south of England, as well as her lifelong islomania. It has appeared in *Earthlines*, *The Clearing*, and *Women on Nature*. Her academic works include the co-edited *Walking, Landscape and Environment*, the forthcoming co-authored *Modern British Nature Writing 1789–2020: Land Lines*, and a monograph entitled *Ecocriticism and the Island*. She is also a musician and songwriter, represented by Real World Music Publishing.

Photo © Harry Shepherd

ZAKIYA MCKENZIE is a PhD candidate with the Leverhulme Trust-supported Caribbean Literary Heritage project at the University of Exeter researching Black British journalism in the post-war period. Zakiya is a writer and storyteller and was the 2019 writer-in-residence for Forestry England during its centenary year. In Bristol, she was 2017 Black and Green Ambassador and is a volunteer at Ujima Community Radio station. She regularly leads nature, art and writing workshops, including one on Caribbean storytelling for primary schools. Her work has featured at the Cabot Institute for the Environment at the University of Bristol, the Institute for Modern Languages Research at the University of London, the Hepworth Wakefield Gallery, the Free Word Centre, at Cheltenham Literature Festival, and on the BBC's *Woman's Hour*, *Farming*

Today and *Inside Out West* programmes. She has written for *Smallwoods* magazine, *The Willowherb Review* and the BBC's *Wildlife* magazine. http://zakiya.me

Photo © Ranju Roy

ANITA ROY is a writer, editor and publisher of mixed British and Indian heritage. She spent twenty years living and working in New Delhi, until returning to the UK in 2015. Her essays have appeared in *Granta*, *Guernica*, *The Clearing*, *Outlook Traveller*, *India Quarterly* and *Dark Mountain* among others. She is the author of a children's fantasy adventure, *Gravepyres School for the Recently Deceased*, a picture book, *The Power of Ten*, and a nature diary *A Year at Kingcombe: The Wildflower Meadows of Dorset*. She holds an MA in Travel and Nature Writing from Bath Spa University, and is a regular contributor to the *Guardian* Country Diary column. She lives with her son in Somerset. www.anitaroy.net

Photo © Humans of Leeds

TESTAMENT is an acclaimed rapper, playwright and world-record-holding beatboxer based in West Yorkshire. His work includes the hip-hop album *Homecut: No Freedom Without Sacrifice*, spoken word performances for radio and television and the celebrated play *Black Men Walking* (nominated for Best Play at The Writer's Guild Awards 2019 and Best New Play at the UK Theatre Awards 2020). His radio play *The Beatboxer* was nominated for the Imison Award at the BBC Audio Drama Awards 2020. Testament was Channel 4 Writer in Residence at Royal Exchange Theatre Manchester and his show *Orpheus in the Record Shop* was broadcast on BBC Four in 2021. Testament's writing has been published in several anthologies and has been used as a teaching resource internationally.

Photo © Elizabeth Reeder

AMANDA THOMSON is a visual artist and writer who is also a lecturer at the Glasgow School of Art. Her writing has appeared in *The Willowherb Review*, *Gutter* and the anthology *Antlers of Water: Writing on the Nature and Environment of Scotland*, edited by Kathleen Jamie. She earned her doctorate in interdisciplinary arts practice, based around the landscapes and the forests of the North of Scotland, in 2013. She lives and works in Strathspey, in the Scottish Highlands, and Glasgow. Her first book, *A Scots Dictionary of Nature*, is published by Saraband Books; and a collaboration with Elizabeth Reeder, *microbursts*, a collection of lyric and intermedial essays, was published by Prototype Publishing in February 2021. She is currently working on her second book.

Photo © Eva Vermandel

LUKE TURNER'S critically acclaimed memoir *Out of the Woods* – a reflection on sexuality, masculinity and the relationship between humans and 'nature' – was his first book. It was shortlisted for the 2019 Wainwright Prize for nature writing, and longlisted for the Polari Prize for first book by an LGBT+ writer. He has participated in collaborative exhibitions at the V&A, Hayward and Serpentine Galleries. He is co-founder and editor of *The Quietus* and writes for a variety of publications including the *Guardian*, *Observer*, *Vice*, *Dazed & Confused*, *National Geographic*, *NME*, and the *SomeSuch* journal, and has appeared on BBC Radio Three, Four and 6Music, as well as television programmes. He is currently writing a new book about masculinity, sexuality and the Second World War.

Acknowledgements

First and foremost, we thank Rupert Lancaster for having the vision to commission *Gifts of Gravity and Light*, and the whole team at Hodder and Stoughton for working with us so generously and creatively on the collection.

Zack Mclaughlin is an artist who works wonders with paper and wood: his kestrel – or 'windhover' as it's sometimes known – graces the cover of this book. The care, love and painstaking work that have gone into each feather have lifted our spirits and given us wings. We thank him and the designers at Hodder for their creativity.

We are hugely grateful to Bernardine Evaristo, an untiring champion of diversity in writing, for her inspirational foreword; to the Poet Laureate, Simon Armitage, who offered us his support from the very outset of this project and graciously gave us permission to take words from his poem 'You're Beautiful' for our title and to reprint the lines from his translation of *Sir Gawain and the Green Knight* to conclude the volume; and to Scotland's former Makar, Jackie Kay, for allowing us to use her beautiful 'Promise' as our epigraph.

Heartfelt thanks to our authors, who took the writers' brief and flew with it, and whose brilliant words surpassed all expectations and were true gifts of gravity and light in a dark year.

We would like to honour the work done by Jessica J. Lee, founder of *The Willowherb Review*, the online platform for emerging and established nature writers of colour, along with the Nan Shepherd Prize, and the Nature Writing Prize for Working Class Writers, all of which are helping to raise the profile of under-represented voices in nature writing. Several of our authors have been published in *The Willowherb Review*, while Michael Malay was shortlisted for the Nan Shepherd Prize. We salute the long-standing organisations involved with nature writing who are working towards greater inclusivity in their awards and festival programmes.

Anita would like to thank: Stephen Moss for his unfailingly generous encouragement along the way; Simon Leach for shedding light on all things tilted and equinoctial; Derek Augarde for his trust – and a key; and the extended Roy family clan for absolutely everything else.

Pippa would like to thank: the Land Lines team at the University of Leeds, and colleagues at the University of Bristol Centre for Environmental Humanities; Mark Birkinshaw, Professor of Cosmology and Astrophysics at the University of Bristol, for talking her through solar and sidereal time and the precession of the spring equinox – any errors remain, of course, her own; Steven, Michael and Anita, the brilliant Musketeers; and, as always, with love, Andrew, Katie and Lily.

Text Acknowledgements

Jackie Kay's 'Promise' from *Darling: New & Selected Poems* (2007) is reprinted with the permission of Bloodaxe Books.

In '*Equinox*: I Put this Moment', the excerpt from 'Jig of Life' (words and Music by Kate Bush © 1985) is reproduced by permission of Noble & Brite Ltd/ Sony Music Publishing, London W1T 3LP; Robert Bush's daughter's reminiscence is from a BBC World War One at Home programme *Knoll Hill, Bristol: Bishop's Knoll War Hospital*; the quotation from Michel Cassé is taken from his *Stellar Alchemy: The Celestial Origin of Atoms* (Cambridge: CUP, 2003); and the essay drew on the *New York Times* article 'A Pregnancy Souvenir: Cells That Are Not Your Own' (10 September, 2015) for details of microchimerism.

In 'Your Shrouded Form', the poem 'Autumn' and other excerpts from the poetry and prose of Siegfried Sassoon are copyright Siegfried Sassoon and used by kind permission of the Estate of George Sassoon.

In 'It's Hopping Time', the extracts of Raine Geoghegan's poetry are taken from her collections *Apple Water: Povel Panni* (2018) and *They Lit Fires: Lenti Hatch o Yog* (2019) and reprinted with permission from Hedgehog Poetry Press.

The extract from Simon Armitage's *Sir Gawain and the Green Knight* and the phrase 'gifts of gravity and light' from 'You're Beautiful' (*Paper Aeroplanes: Selected Poems 1989–2014*) are used with permission from Faber and Faber Ltd.